My World

K. Charles Latimer

DayMares

&

NightDreams

K. Charles Latimer

DayMares & NightDreams

Kenneth C. Latimer
309. E. Mills Ave.
El Paso Texas. 79901
(915) 990-6254
E-mail; selrahc717@hotmail.com

DayMares

&

NightDreams

K. Charles Latimer

I dedicate this book to: Ophelia Thompson,
my grandmother.

Rest in Heaven, for you deserve it.

Chapter One

How do you sum up a person's life in just one poem or even one book? Our lives are a couple of volumes, at the least. We go through so many things, so many hurts and so many changes in our lives that we can't write enough pages to describe it. However, just like this book, it does give the reader an insight on whom and what the author is about. This is what I'm attempting to do with this book.

Here's the irony of this, those that grew up with me and family members that I share my childhood with probably know less than those that read this collection of my thoughts.

Being the youngest of seven children, I have always felt that my thoughts and feelings were less important than my siblings. Maybe, it was just my imagination, but I have experienced things, during my childhood, that has adversely affected me as an adult. And if you read my autobiography titled; The Reconstruction of Me, then you will know even more of the story and again, maybe, you will understand my poetry and thoughts that I have written here.

Like with all artist, their work says more about them than what anyone see from them. Because, as an artist, it is easier to voice your thoughts on a canvas, in a sculpture, in a song or on paper than voicing it to anyone. I have always, since a child, hid my feelings, hid my thoughts and emotions, because I thought no one cared. As I got older, I started to voice my feelings on paper just for my personal relief and as I wrote my poems, I begin to believe that I was pretty good at this. After reading this book, you may have your own opinion of my talents, but I believe that I'm good at this and that's all that matters to me.

However, I hope that you read, enjoy and maybe even, learn something from what I have wrote. There's even a thought that you may see yourself in my writings and relate and will see yourself in a different light. That's my intentions, my purpose and my reason for this book.

The first couple of poems are more spiritual then anything. These came at a time when I had just confessed my belief in the Lord and sought to become a minister. God was giving me thoughts of revelation that was only for me and if these thoughts help someone else then that would be good because my job as a minister, from the Bible's explanation, is to administer, hence the word minister, the word of God. But we, as people, children of God, are to hand out, deliver the word to others, so if you are doing that, you are a minister, whether a paper or document proclaims you as such or not. Continue to spread His word no matter what anyone says but be wise in the word before you display it. And do me one favor, ask God for revealing knowledge before you talk because as the word says; "Lean not on your own understanding."

There's also one more point that I want to make. We need to stop calling ourselves, as children of God, Christians because, if you know the bible, there is nowhere in there that Christ said that you were a Christian or to call yourself a Christian. King Agrippa was the first to use this word and he used it as a curse word not as a badge of honor. Some may say that the Apostle Paul said that we are Christian but that not what he said. He simply stated that if this was the title or label that you put on me, then so be it. Again, he's not saying that we should call ourselves that but if those who don't believe want to call us that then let them. Christ, throughout the New Testament, never says you are or should be known as Christians. He plainly states, follower, disciples, children of God and even my people but he never used the word Christian. But like I always say, 'Don't take my word, look it up for yourself.'

My World   K. Charles Latimer

    Well I hope you enjoy my poems and again, I
want them to inspire, lift up and strengthen you.
Live, Learn and Love.

A Tua Bocca
(In Your Mouth)

Just as you are, come to Him.
For He enables you to.
Evoke the power you possess.
It's all up to you.
Rest peacefully in His glory,
Venture willingly into His pastures.
Enter the grace and goodness of God,
Exclaim that He is your Master.
Most loving and gracious to all of us,
Filling us with His Mighty Spirit.
Inside of only those who ask,
Ones whose heart truly desires it.
Authority has been given
Upon us as heavenly heirs.
Hades and all that dwell there,
Remains feeble in their lair.
There's something that's within you,
Even the saint of heaven lack.
Embedded in you is a fire,
Now the Word of God is your match.

Recount, "The Way"

Problems in life are a constant battle.
Trials and tribulation take their toll.
Rat races of the world leave us strapped and
weary,
Have us begging, "Have mercy on my soul."
On the front line in this battle of the spirit,
Ready and poised are the principalities of the dark.
Viciously wielding their evil weapons at you,
Eager to destroy, as they hit their mark.
Entangled in a web of lust, hate and guilt.
Effecting our ways which are easily seen.
Recounting the things that got you this way,
Succumbing to the flesh man and his filth.
But remember, to those who walk in His way,
Inside you there's a peace you can trust.
Submitting all things to His mighty hands,
X-acting the Lord as you must.

Return To Me.

Elation, joy and contentment you will feel,
Once you step into the fold.
Praise the Lord with thanksgiving,
Newness of life you will hold.
Here on out, you're never alone.
Elevate your voice and be bold.
Easy to say; "Dear Lord save me,"
So that He may ease the load.
Settle in His warm embrace,
Else remain in the dark where it's cold.
I can tell you about the works of His hand,
Verily, just as I was told.
And His great sacrifice, of His Son Jesus Christ,
Enduring to buy back our souls.
Nailed to the cross, for Satan had lost,
Never knew redemption was Gods goal.
Saving us all from sin to which we were sold.

Ride the Light

Join in on an amazing journey.
One you have never experienced before.
The way that you go is very well lit.
However, there's only one Door.
We've searched our lives for an adventure like this,
Now available, we wonder what to do.
ELOHAY has given us a way like no other.
Endure and you will get thought.
Life eternal you'll get going down this path,
In the Light that shines brightly upon it.
Vanity awaits, if you choose not to venture,
Graves of darkness is where you will sit.
Escapades of joy, goodness and glory,
Had by all those who are willing.
The ride of your life, the Light of Christ,
It's sure to leave you reeling.

Yah Knows !

Inside every person,
There's a battle raging fierce.
Some may say its fear,
While others deny that it exists.
Are we so fickle in our hearts?
Even in the recesses of our thoughts,
In believing on he who created us.
Lest we think we will be without.
All he has made belongs to you.
Victory, we have, over all the wiles of evil.
He has placed His Son on the cross for us.
Enlighten us with His Spirit.
Trusting His ways, we should all yearn to do.
With our hearts and minds alike.
Omniscience is not just a phrase.

No Sleeves Required

Few have given love beyond the boundaries of the
heart that beats within.
Only the physical love that mankind's shows that
we gauge what and how
it is revealed.
In the blink of an eye that love we have come to
know fizzles out of
existence.
Nevertheless, we continue to search for amore' a
new as if we were healed.
Repeating this habitual process in life some think is
for the best.
Evidently, those whom say such things are mostly
alone themselves for
misery loves company.
Seeing our hearts drizzled upon those whom dare
to go sleeveless and seem
to know our words to the letter
Sounds of pitying melodrama concur with
abundance on any noonday
symphony.
Take stock in yourself with remembrance of the
blessed glow that Christ
have given, which you are wasting.

My World   K. Charles Latimer

Excel past all the worlds trivial pains that keeps us
enslaved in our earthly
emotions.
Jubilee in the ample showers of crimson that every
sheep in the fold should
be tasting.
Vintage essence pressed from the vineyards of His
cross, so consume it
with devotion.
Offering our hearts to Christ Jesus is far wiser than
falling prey to mans
limited love.
Enjoy an earnest yearning for a life in His will and
His Word.
Have your whole being washed, not by the blood of
goats and calves,
but by His blood from above.
Nay the service or advice of the sleeved ones be
needed, nor will you
venture for it to be heard.
Nothing compares to the glow of newness you will
receive after you are
cleansed of your sins by Christ.

Chapter Two

During this time of spiritual awaking, I had several thoughts that helped me along the way. As I read the bible, the Lord gave me a certain enlightenment, which raised my level of spiritual understanding. With the strengthening of my revelation knowledge I have grown in my life, to a point, where I do realize other troubles, other problems and thoughts. This helped me to really understand and minister to those that were in need. It aided in how the Lord uses me and how He worked through me. Therefore, this chapter is so different than the first one.

As I have gone through my share of pain and heartaches, I have grown in, not only my knowledge, but in my wisdom as a person and a man. These trials have strengthened me, as yours have for you, and has forced me to see things in a different light. However, no two people have the exact same pain, nor the same happiness, so we must, as human beings, not categorize situations in life as the same. I have learned this as I have grown in my ministry and my dealings with people. However, I must say that there are three things that no person can escape nor deny. I call them the three 'L's' of being human. These three things are Lies, Lust and being Lucrative. These where instilled in us from our very creation and are part of why we live, succeed and our happiness. Without these three elements, we would have no desire, no diplomacy and this world would not have grown as it has.

Some may say that this is just not true or that it is an excuse for our wrong doings, but I say that our wrong doings are what makes us the very beings that the Lord created from the start. The Lord distilled these very iniquities in us for us to grow, flourish and survive. **The growth of mankind is not solely based on their goodness but is cultivated from their deceit and greed.**

Let's me explain each one, in more detail, maybe you will understand better and hopefully agree. We will start with the most obvious and controversial one, **Lies.** We, as humans, believe strongly that our moral compass guides us correctly, unfortunately and blindly, it destroys the very fabric of this morality daily. Even though we proclaim to others and believe within ourselves that we are truthful at every turn, we lie to ourselves and those we love constantly. But here's the thing, it is not the lie that vilifies us, it the intention of it that cause the hurt and pain. Example, if someone were to asks; 'how are you doing', your immediate response will be, 'fine' even though you may be having a bad day. But this lie harms no one and its initial intentions are not to damage anyone, all the same, it is a lie none the less. Whether you call it a 'little white lie', 'a slight bending of the truth', or a 'minor deception', it is still a lie.

Even if we, let's say, went out to lunch with an ex of ours, even though we knew that our current spouse despises them. The lunch was harmless, innocent and without any sexual thoughts or tensions. But when our current spouse asks you where you were, most people will lie to avoid the drama and argument. Now the intentions here are, from your aspect, for the greater good but when your spouse finds out about it, all hell breaks loose. The right and wrongs about this is a conversation for another day and another book, but my point is that, even with good intentions, we lie. Yet we profess our honor of being truthful and stand proudly on our morality of honesty.

Now, if we, in the previous situation, met a person with the intentions of having an intimate relationship with and deceive the current person that we are in a relationship with, then that's a whole different matter. This is a lie with known hurtful ramifications. Even though, in our own mind, we will justify this as a beneficial misconception to keep the status quo. Difference being, as you know, with the first one there was no infidelity and with the other, infidelity was the initial intention. I understand the opposite values in both examples however it's still a lie regardless of the circumstance. Our human morality will try to put a logical spin on this, but reality will categorize this as it would the other two examples. A lie is a lie, regardless how and why it's told. Good intentions or not, it's a lie, a dishonest display of the truth and a misconception of reality.

Next, there's **Lust.** Merriam-Webster dictionary defines this as a 'personal inclination or an unusual intense or unbridle desire.', however, we humanly pin-point this to a more sexual inclination and that's the road I will take during my explanation. We, as men and women, again, claim that we are above reproach when it comes to this aspect of our values. We like to believe that we do not and would not adhere to this grossly inherent trait. But before I explain this, again, let's go back to the definition, which states that this is a 'personal inclination' and that means it's a simple thought. Now, we all have seen someone, whether on T.V., or in real life, that we have found attractive. Even though the thought of having sex with them is out of the picture, we still have the idea that they are sexy, desirable and excites that area in us we try not to voice. This basic and humanly inclination is thought to be unsavory, unchristian-like and boorish. Just like a lie, it's the intentions that will make it a good or bad thing. And it is by these intentions, when acted upon, gives lust its horrendous reputation. Lust is in the very essence of our creation. It was and has been embedded in us at our creation. We see and learn this from the story of Adam and Eve. As much as we try to fight, dismiss and believe that we are beyond this, we still find ourselves falling prey to this powerful yet simple desire.

The power of Lust is that our loins have an uncontrollable yearning, an inherit attraction and an embedded need to copulate. But we must realize that we cannot band this, bond this or simply biblically control this because one of the major things that God told Adam is to be fruitful and multiply. And how was he to do that but to copulate. So, for him to do this, Lust had to be a factor. Desire had to be a factor. Now, we would all like to sexually engage with the one we love however reality gives us something different. As a youth, I wanted to be with the one I loved or my true soul mate, but life gave me what my loins desired, at that moment and time. She was not the everlasting love that I wished for, but she was the sexual release that I needed at that time. Even today, at the wise age of 55, I still fall to the desires of Lust, as I believe we all do.

Last, but not least, is being **Lucrative.** We all know this as, benefitting from the work that we have done. Receiving adequate compensation for one's talents, skills or abilities is the very fiber that this free country was built on. We ask, request, and sometimes, demand this simple yet basic principle.

My World   K. Charles Latimer

Wars have been fought and people have died for this. Inventions were discovered, companies have thrived, and economies grew by man's desire to become lucrative. This element is often mistaken for greed however, even though greed maybe a driving force in some cases, it's not the intentional factor behind the biblical principle of 'reaping what you sow.' Mankind infused greed into this innocent and natural request that the Lord instilled in us. Nowadays, being lucrative is known as a bad thing because the first thing we hear is greed. I admit, with my writing, I would love to be lucrative from it, and by growing up in this era of prosperity, greed does enter my mind. Don't get me wrong, I write because I love it and it gives me a chance to voice my thoughts. But it would be nice to have a best-selling book and I believe, if I continue to write, it will happen. However, I'm no different than the person that goes to work every day and dreams that they will move up the ranks and earn more money, or the person that plays the lottery in hopes to hit it big. We all have aspirations of being lucrative in anything that we do. Again, we may love what we do and making money may not be the driving force for what we do but, it is an element.

But back to my point, and hopefully you can see, that these three 'L's', **Lie**, **Lust** and being **Lucrative** are just part of who we are as humans. And those

that say they do not fall prey to these attribute,
just became a victim of the very first one. However,
I'm a realist and these next poems will reveal my
battles with these three. Enjoy.

Accolades, A Misconception.

There is a place and a position, in society, for all
things and all feelings.
Even though we ignore the emotions that are
considered as taboo,
Such mental thoughts as hate, jealousy, envy and
greed come to mind.
But we, as being human, must acknowledge these
aspects of life too.
We run from them as if they do not reside in the
essence of our very being.
And we assume that we are greater them sum of
these intricate parts.
Yet these elements are greater than we want to
believe.
For they are and forever will be embedded in our
hearts.
There is nothing that we successfully do that we
refuse to take claim to.
However, our front of modesty, seem to supersede
the truth.
So, we banish the thoughts that we have done
something great.
And concede our accomplishment to our own little
booth.
Our accolades are the driving force in life that
makes us who we are.

My World   K. Charles Latimer

Without this no inventor would have created what
we know now.
Edison would not have continued his path of
illumination.
If within his mind he was not seeking an accepted
bow.
Accolades are why we do what we do and who we
have become.
But we dismiss it and hide this emotion for it's not
politically correct.
Thus, we claim this is not what we seek but deep in
us the elements hides.
As the promises of our ventures dissipate, seems
that everyone can detect.
Accolades make fame and fame makes money and
that is our forethought.
And in this world, unfortunately, money seems to
possess the power to rule.
Because in this existence it holds us, commands us
and directs our very path.
So, with the force of accolades, that we so desire,
we are only just a tool.
We make money, we create money and we live
based on our accolades.
We live, we breathe, we invent, and we survive
because of this purpose.
Some may say that we are the creation of our will
and ingenuity.
But I simply say that we are just the implements of
accolades surplus.

Don De La Vida
(Gift of Life)

What does the heart owe?
Some may say peace.
Others command their share of joy.
What about your issue of happiness?
Surely love, the heart can make so.
Those are just glorious benefits,
Or sometimes the pursuit is the liability.
No doubt we want these things,
And to some degree, they are needs,
But if it doesn't fit then don't force it.
However, it's not the hearts payment,
Nor is it a bill that's past due.
Its rhythmic beats pay the toll,
And distribution is the job description,
Without a weekly statement.
We receive life, and that is vital.
A gift that's given to all.
To which some don't even open,
Let alone venture to use.
So, allow the heart to do the chore not our title.
Because without life the wants are fickle.

My World   K. Charles Latimer

Without life the needs are null.
Liabilities become non-existent,
And benefits are not worth a nickel.
Life gives us a desire to love and exchange.
Life experiences gather joy.
Happiness can be had by savoring life.
And peace comes as you settle into life.
So, we owe the heart our change.
But cash, check or credit is not legal tender.
To pay, love all as you do oneself,
Engulf the joy of your very presence.
Let happiness reign in all you do,
Then the comfort of peace will rain down its
splendor.
Ergo, pay the heart its due.
Stop waiting on it to pay you.
You've got the gift of life,
Now unwrap it and use it.

It's Our World

We Live, we cry, we laugh.
Life fills us with emotions.
We steal, we hurt, and we lie.
Life is a basket of commotion.
How do we sort these files?
Do we download an app?
Should we just erase them?
Or do we come strapped?
On Facebook and twitter,
We post all our thoughts.
Do we stream with our voice?
Or do we let it go naught?
I believe this is the era to let our feelings be known.
And to let our thoughts stand strong.
Whether you agree or disagree,
Good or bad, right or wrong.
Let your voice come forth,
And let be known your opinion.
Stand fast on your beliefs,
And move not, on your decisions.
Adults do evolve to better solutions,
We may even shop at a different store
But being grown makes you wise,
But we never stray from the core.

My World   K. Charles Latimer

Age doesn't make you know it all,
But it does give you a template.
On how to live your life.
And to make you great.

JOY OF ....

Summer blows its breath upon all that is before,
after and on you.
In the solace of the day the celestial ember coats
your very essences.
Ecstasy is in the fragrances propelled by the
inhabitants of the season.
The caress of good feelings that intoxicate all by
the presence of the sun.
As a family, we gather, as neighbors we connect, as
a nation, we combined.
We share ourselves, our culinary aromas and
talents for all to enjoy.
Weddings, reunions and all events are made extra
special by the solar reign.
The laughter of kids play, the peace of the park, the
mood of the mountains.
This is the joy of summer.
With hearts all a flutter when you see each other as
the body temp rises.
A grasp of their hand and there you will stand
afraid to miss the moment.
A delicate stroke of their face then your lips
embraces to set ablaze the embers within.
Explosions of emotion as you are confused by the
commotion of your intellect being scrambled like
an egg.

My World   K. Charles Latimer

Your daily life is in hell but with them you can
exhale yet first you must inhale all that they hold.
Two bodies merging as one with eager anticipation
to come inside their lives forever.
A soothing sweat bead your brow and you are
certain by now that this is your destiny.
This is the joy of love.
With this test there were no mathematics involve
yet you received a plus.
Your heart race with elation as you realized your
eggs have been seeded.
The joyous news has been spread and even the
father was full of excitement.
Nine months are just a blur but now the moment
has come for new life.
Pain now is just a bridge that enters an elated road
of creation.
A piercing cry hits the air as if trumpets sounding
its arrival to the world.
At that moment time is on a speedy course that at
a blink you could miss.
First word, first steps, first school, first car, first
date and then that aisle.
You sit there and wonder where the time went as
you proudly let them go.
This is the joy of children.
All this that has been said is an element in our
heads and we hold these truths to be evident.
With each awakening of the dawn we find a reason
to go on for hopes like these is our fuel.

My World   K. Charles Latimer

The memories of these times bring peace to our
minds letting us know there is a bigger picture.
What ever faith we believe or whatever thoughts
we conceive, we breathe, and others breathe
through us.
As we go through day to day and no matter what
you may say, it's our choice to create the picture.
So, whether good or bad, happy or sad we made it
and we can change it.
Let the good you feel be for real and the bad be
your effort to correct.
Know that there is better thing there because you
are aware that it exists.
This is the joy of life.

My Goodness

Breath your breathe and bless me Lord
Lift me up, fill me with your love.
Give me the answers that I need.
And bring me to the heavens above.
Love me Lord for I know I don't deserve it.
Cover me with your cloth of goodness
Carry me Lord for I know I haven't earned it
Bless me with your power
In your word I will live
Because I know your love you will show
With my praise, I know you will give.
Take my life and make it whole.
Lay your heavenly hands on me.
Remove the blinders from my eyes,
And now I can see.
Strengthen me oh Lord,
This life has broken me.
With your grace and mercy,

O' Mountain, My Mountain.

O' mountain, my mountain, why do you haunt me
so?
The grandeur of your presence shakes me to my
core.
With fear, I wonder, how can I over take you.
As your massive peaks rise and your width seems
no end.
O' mountain, my mountain, from afar your guise is
humble and meek.
Even to the point of beauty and glory.
But the closer I get, you make my knees grow
weak.
Which recalls a much more ominous story.
O' mountain, my mountain, human nature tells me
to traverse you.
But with your ridges and gullies, I know that's not
the path for me.
So, I sit there feeling weakened, not knowing
where to go.
A still small voice says; "Over is not your route. You
must go through."
O' mountain, my mountain, as I get back on the
path and venture ahead.
I am engulfed by your darkness, as you surround
me.
The Lord says; 'By faith' I have the power to move
you.

My World   K. Charles Latimer

So, I will stand firm and fast on this Word, as I
tread.
O' mountain, my mountain, now I see the light, as I
go through.
I feel the warmth of the sun and the fresh air
envelopes me.
But just ahead I see another mountain, standing
ready to shake.
O' mountain, my mountain, thru Christ, now I know
what to do.

My Heaviest Burden

Much of what you see from me is what you get.
Years, no decades, brought me to this point.
But the travesties of my passenger weakened me.
And yet the damage is still done, to all I've met.
Together we have caused pain because I have let
him win.
Then comes morn, as the shadows of my battle
come to light.
Leaning on whatever logic I can display.
Even though, I know the wages of this sin.
Within me, I know, lay the power to put him aside.
I constantly argue with him, as I drive.
Then I see the weight of him, makes it hard to put
him out.
However, with every obstacle, he convinces me to
let him ride.
Animosity, hatred and fear are the few words to
describe him.
Least of all co-pilot, which he is far from being.
Coming into my golden years, I should be wise
enough to depart.
Only to fall prey to him, as the lights go dim.

My World   K. Charles Latimer

Heavenly Father, I pray to get MaGilla out my
backseat.
Out of my mind, off my heart and under my feet.
Leaving him dormant, weaken and in defeat.
If left inside of me, there's no way I can't compete.
So, grant this request, for the many and not the
few.
My heaviest burden, Dear Lord, I give to you.

It's Time.

I've heard all the punchlines.
From; 'Ask not' to 'Make America Great'.
I'm just waiting to hear the truth.
No rhetoric……give it to me straight.
I'm not fragile, weak or dumb.
Give me the real, cause I can take it.
Pull the covers off America.
For I've grown weary of the bullshit.
Tell me the gov is all about themselves.
That the rich will only get richer.
That the poor will continue to be ignored.
And that our well-being lay waste on shelves.
Kennedy played civil rights, like a political tool.
Which LBJ was forced to pass.
Nixon treated the House like a joke.
And Ford was just a drive-by with no gas.
Carter grinned his way to these nuts.
And Reagan fooled us by trickling down.
Bush clipped us by; 'No new taxes'.
However, Clinton gave us a surplus, as repubs
frowned.
It only took 8yrs for G.Dub to put us in the pits.
To which Obama brought us out of.
And with the outcome of the latest election,
Trump will put us back in the shit.
When will America shake its head and wake up?

My World   K. Charles Latimer

This is just a game and we are the pawns.
The gov never intended for us to win.
They just played one group against the other like
prawns.
We the people, are supposed to have the power.
But like a limp sword, it has no force.
All the power we have will come to naught.
If we don't come together with one voice.
I love this country, even though, at times, it doesn't
love me.
Or put me on an equal playing field.
Whether you are black, red, yellow or brown.
We should never have to yield.
But if we don't drop this superiority complex.
And live and love together as one.
We, as a world, will be the destruction of
ourselves.
To which, mankind itself, will cease to exist.
Before us, in this era, lay a testing ground.
So, what do we do with it?
Will our frivolous egos lay waste our good morals?
Or allow debauchery to consume us to it's pits.
I, for one, believe mankind is better than this.
God created us all with the same sense, blood and
life.
But it's only by the power of His love.
That we will defeat hate, pain, and strife.

Chapter Three

There was this young man who was fighting in the Vietnam War. And one night, as they were out on maneuvers, he stepped on a landmine and was seriously wounded. For weeks, he was heavily sedated, and his condition was very questionable. Finally, he regained consciousness and a throbbing pain began in his legs. As he looked around, slightly groggy, for a nurse or a doctor to help, but they were all hustling about tending to the other patients. After a few minutes, his pain got so unbearable that he yelled out in agony, "Someone please help me!"

Quickly, a nurse came over to see about him and he told her how much pain he was in. He informed her that the pain in his legs was excruciating and pleaded for her to give him pain reducer. The nurse seemed puzzled, so she called over the doctor. By this time, the young man was angrily yelling out orders for pain medicine. The doctor tried to calm him down but to no success. Then finally, after getting the young man attention, the doctor simply said; "Son, it's impossible for you to be having pains in your legs." Then the doctor pulled the covers back and finished by saying; "because you don't have any legs."

In medical terminology, this is known as 'Phantom Pains', which is defined as being hindered by something that is not there. This is a mental ailment that could not be possible, because the pain that the patient is feeling is impossible for the limb, or extremity no longer exist. However, pain is still present, but only in the patients' mind. In the Book of Acts, chapter 3 verses 1-10; "'Now Peter and John went up together to the temple at the hour of prayer, the ninth hour. And a certain man, lamed from his mother's womb, was carried and laid daily at the gate of the temple, which was called Beautiful, to ask alms from those that entered the temple, who, seeing Peter and John about to go into the temple, ask for alms. And fixing his eyes on him, John and Peter said; "Look at us." So, he gave them his attention, expecting to receive something from them. Them Peter said; "Silver and gold, I do not have, but what I do have, I give you. In the name of Jesus Christ of Nazareth, rise up and walk." And he took him by the right hand and lifted him up, and immediately his feet and ankle bones received strength. So, he leaped up, stood and walked and entered the temple with them, walking, leaping and praising God. Then they knew that it was he that sat begging for alms at the Beautiful Gate of the temple, and they were filled with wonder and amazement at what had happened to him,"' (NKJV)

Let's examine this scripture for a moment, starting with verse 2. It says that the man was lame and disable from his mother's womb. A lot of us are disable or handicapped at birth, but it's only a limitation. But here is a difference. To be disabled or handicapped, is not being able to do what you use to or thought you could normally do. A limitation is where you are capable but mentally, you feel that you can't. Limitations are more mental than physical, because a limit is something that we can exceed or go beyond. A limitation is something that is set by someone else, or even by the individual themselves. Keep this in mind, as we continue this story.

This man was disabled and was carried, daily, to the front of the gates of the temple called Beautiful. Here, he would ask for alms or beg for money. He begged because of his disability, but unfortunately, a lot of people today do the same thing because of their felt limitations. Remember, when a person is begging for something, they get down on their knees committing or submitting themselves to a lesser state, and begging for something that they think they don't have.

In the Book of John, 1:3, it states; "All things were made through Him and without Him, nothing was made." Also, in Romans 8:16-17 it says: "The Spirit bears witness tour spirit, that we are children of God, and if children's, then heirs of God, joint heirs with Christ. If indeed we suffer with Him. That we may also be glorified together." And let me also add 2nd Peter 1:3, which says; "His divine power has given us all thing that pertain to life and godliness, through the knowledge of Him, who called us by glory and virtue,"

These next poems are about the futility of mankind and the emptiness we suffer daily. I ask you to let these words give you pause to evaluate what, when and who you are as a person. Let the words touch the very heart of you and ignite a spirit that you thought was long gone.

Inevitability

It will take you, hold you, caress you and make its
all.
Love the tender touch of its goodness.
Inevitability.
Let it will you into its light, goodness and warmth.
Let the sunshine upon your presence and enjoy it.
Allow the warming rays of the solar embrace engulf
you.
It will guide you and lead you to your radiant bliss.
You've become a slave to the enticing rapture of its
existence.
You can't resist how its heat soothes the very
essence of your being.
Inevitability.
Yet you cry; "Solar gods please release me and let
me be free."
Begging; "Unmold me, release my mind and allow
me to breath."
"Trust me, I love your touch but you are selfish"
"You know that I need you but you have the upper
hand."
Inevitability.
"Why do you pull the chains on me?"
"My life has no meaning if you are not there."
"As I plant, I depend on you to help me grow."
"Yet your sunrays have me in its clutch."
Inevitability.
Then the night comes and I pray for your presence.
Inevitability.

Dead Heads

There's no brown out.
Electricity slows to a crawl.
Windows to the soul, closed.
While trap doors seep fluid.
The Dead Head appears.
Leaning, leaning, leaning.
Falling, falling, falling,.
But never falls.
All is scattered but still intact.
Broken, battened and disarray.
The Dead Head darkens.
Molly, Mary and Dick come to play,
And they pull the puppet strings.
Two bones, pay for the tow.
To the shadows, hence you stand.
Dead Head, is no dictator.
You elected him.

A Leaf

Like life, it changes.
And like life, the end is a new.
But still there is pain.
Just live for the new.
Yet life is gonna happen,
So love who you are.
Let your green flourish and grow.
And know, when it falls that it will grow again.

Ripples of the Crowd

Have you heard the roar of the crowd?
The cheers of the many.
The influence from the populous.
Does this not weigh heavy on you?
To allow the harrows of your thoughts,
Change the rivers that flow.
Release yourself from the umbilical waters of the
past.
Restrain the ravenous learning by the hounds of
hell.
Engulf yourself in the beatitudes of generations
before.
And give into the proprieties of the heart.
Give effort to yield to the purity of humanity.
Our innards are not born to animosity and fear.
Nor is it derived from hatred and greed.
That is our outer shell we fall prey to.
We are initially made of kindness and goodness.
Our essence is comprised with respect and love.
Yet the gaggle tweaks our insecurities, leading us
astray.
Lo those who beckon the call of the many.
Lo those that seek comfort from the despaired.

My World   K. Charles Latimer

However, raise yourself beyond the depths of
worldly duplicities.
Reach out for your coup de maître.
Let the roots of kindness infuse the inert element
of agape.
For he whom swims in the ripples of the many,
Is often drowned by the lack of belief in himself.

Believe In The Best,

Love is great to give and get.
It softens our hearts and soothes our minds.
And opens us up to the wonders in life.
Allowing us to feel sympathy for all mankind.
But there's another emotion just as strong.
It's like closing a door, with no worries of the rest.
My love for you, no one can compare.
However, for you and I, I only believe in the best.
If the world shatters your dreams,
Like it has a tendency to do.
Know that my belief in you excels all things.
No matter where, how and what you go thru.
With you, I have a strength yet seen.
Let me lift you up, to help you bare the load.
My shoulders are built for the weight.
I promise, I won't scold, fold or explode.
Because there's another emotion just as strong.
It's like closing a door, with no worries of the rest.
My love for you, no one can compare.
However, for you and I, I only believe in the best.
Let life deal us all the worst hands that it may.
Together, we will bare it like a scaffold.
No path too crooked, no road too rough.
As we walk this course, all the way, your hand I'll
hold.
From the start, you were always in my heart.
Till today, that has not, and will never change.

My World   K. Charles Latimer

Because, I will be there for you, no matter what.
And that promise has no limit or range.
For there's another emotion just as strong.
It's like closing a door, with no worries of the rest.
My love for you, no one can compare.
However, for you and I, I only believe in the best.

Chapter Four

Out of all the vast amount of emotions that we feel, hate, joy, jealousy, sadness, just to name a few, why is it that love seems to be the most difficult, the hardest to obtain and the most difficult to give? We were not born without the aspect to give this simple emotion and give it abundantly. So what happened from the time we are born to the time when we get into our middle teens? Because that seems to be the moments where we push our ability to give and receive love, further and further back in our minds and hearts. It seems, as if, during this time that we go thru so many emotional changes that, not only ability to love changes, but our very virtue of basic sympathy gets damaged. Now, in the very short period that we have been in existence, and for most people that's about thirteen to fifteen years, will change the way we feel, how we interact and the love we may feel, about people.

Maybe this is because, during these short yet delicate, years we have an explosion of emotions, which is better known as the hormonal burst. Our minds and bodies, in this time, are so confused on how to feel, what to feel and even when to feel it. We have all gone thru this and, as adults, we still are not sure what to do or say about it when our own children go thru it. We try to sympathize or have compassion however, we still end up saying or doing the wrong thing. So we learn that the best thing we can do is to leave them alone and let them go through it. It's a hard thing to see your young person struggling within themselves and you are really powerless to do anything. And we seek solace in the very same people that watched us go thru this very same period.

At the age of 55, I still have difficulties in the element of love and what or who to give to and trust with it. My teenage hormonal bursts are decades past by but the confusion of love still lingers. And with each painful relationship, whether by my doing or not, makes the battle even more difficult to fight, let alone win. But like us all, I don't give up on the hopes of overcoming the

My World   K. Charles Latimer

torturous obstacles of love and to one day get in sync my heart and my mind.

The following poems are a window into my constant battle. Because I've found that through my writings that I can heal, soothe and learn. My hopes are that as you read them, you may also find something that helps you deal with your own personal battle with this beast of burden and joy.

Don De La Vida
(Gift of Life)

What does the heart owe?
Some may say peace.
Others command their share of joy.
What about your issue of happiness?
Surely with love, the heart can make so.
Those are just glorious benefits,
Or sometimes the pursuit is the liability.
No doubt we want these things,
And to some degree, they are needs,
But if it don't fit, then don't force it.
However, it's not the hearts payment,
Nor is it a bill past due.
It's rhythmic beats has paid the toll,
And distribution is its job description,
Without a weekly statement.
We receive life, and that only is vital.
A gift that's given to all.
To which some don't even open,
Let alone, venture to use.
So allow the heart to do the chore as it's made for.
Because without life, the wants are fickle.

My World   K. Charles Latimer

Without life, the needs are null.
Liabilities become non-exsistent,
And the benefits are not worth a nickel.
Life gives us a desire to love and exchange.
Life experiences gather joy.
Happiness can be had by savoring life.
And peace comes as you settle into life.
So we owe the heart for our changes.
But cash, check or credit is not a legal tender.
To pay, love all, as you do oneself.
Engulf the joy of your very presence.
Let happiness reign in all you do.
Then the comforts of peace will rain down its
splendor.
Ergo, pay the hearts its due.
Stop waiting on it to pay you.
You've got the gift of life,
Now unwrap it and use it.

I'm That Man

I'll open the door for you and kiss your hand.
Pull your chair out and buy you roses.
We can picnic in the park.
I'll even nibble your nose.
Whatever romantic thing you want me to do.
I'll hear all your problems because I understand.
With your head on my shoulder, I'll comply.
Fill your heart with joy cause I'm that man.
I'll rub your shoulders and caress your neck.
Lick your breast to make you flex.
Stroke my tongue on your stomach,
And you know what comes next.
Whatever romantic thing you want me to do.
I'll hear all your problems cause I understand.
With your head on my shoulders, I'll comply.
I will love your kids,
But I can't promise I'll be there forever.
Meet the family with grace and charm.
The holidays are good, I won't say never.
Hold you in my embrace to keep you warm.
Make you feel safe in all situations.
Go inside you to make you tremble.
Thinking about me brings intense masturbation.
That makes you wanna groan and mumble.
Whatever romantic thing you want me to do.
I'll hear all your problems, cause I understand.
With your head on my shoulders, I'll comply.
Fill your heart with joy, but marriage, I'm not that
man.

Just Love Me

Will you love me?
Regardless of what I do?
Will you just love me?
For I will do that to you.
Times and troubles can get us all wrapped up.
But with you, I know I'm alive.
Will you just love me?
Because of you I know I can survive.
Will you just love me?
No matter what may come.
Good times, Bad times,
I'll never leave you or run.
Will you just love me?
For I will promise you one thing.
If you always stand by my side,
I will cherish you for life,
And make your heart sing.
Will you just love me?
Because I will always love you.
Spend your life with me.
For I have no life without you.

Only A Tear

Sometimes, only a tear,
Can display a pain others can't see.
Even though, they may not understand,
That drop of moisture can set you free.
Sometimes, only a tear,
Explains the anger that you feel.
A water that cleanses your heart.
To make others know the hurt is real.
Sometimes, only a tear,
Expresses a sign of total joy.
A warmth that spews from our very souls.
As we beam with pride of the success from our girl
or boy.
Sometimes, only a tear,
Reveals the love we really mean.
Our words and acts, maybe cause for deceit.
Yet, a single tear, tells what the heart gleams.
Sometimes, only a tear,
Gives an insight to our pride.
We may not voice our families achievements,
But a single tear shows what's inside.
Sometimes, only a tear.
A single tear.

MAN KIND MAN

Has this genre' of man gone by the way of the
dinosaurs,
And all that remains are fossils to discover?
Also if a women finds one,
He still lacks the vital component of hardness,
Which make him fall short of a complete love-her.
There's an ole saying that seems to ring true.
The kind man, in a race, finishes last.
Even though he may have the fish on his line,
Someone else ends up eating her bass.
However on the other side is mankind.
He can be harsh, vulgar and lite on appreciation.
And a talk of emotion goes over his head.
Together you've created children,
Yet he thinks that raising them is not his station.
Tears are shed and the heart aches,
Which only seems to stiffen his resolve.
With prayers of 'Why won't he change",
'Does he really love me' and 'When will he evolve?'
But in that simple request lays the dilemma.
This makes it difficult for her to understand.
Sometimes in order for him to play what pleases
her ear,
Let him take the baton and conduct the band.
Because a kind man hides his mankind.
And mankind, by pride, loses his kind man.
But like giving birth he can be brought forth.

My World   K. Charles Latimer

With pain, patience and the right gentle hand.
However, a man kind man is still only part of a
man.
Hence the phrase,' the better half.'
Neither is complete without the other.
And together they can live, love and laugh.

SIMPLICITY

Love is plain.
Love is life.
Love is real.
But love is strife.
Love is strong.
Love is bold.
Love is tender.
And love is cold.
Love is pain.
Love is loss.
Realize that.
You know you're not the boss.
Love, it burns.
Love, it stains.
But with true love,
It will always remain.
True love has the power to forgive.
A life of love, is what we should live.
Real love is in our hearts.
Teach your kids from the start.
The world is the water.
And love is the stone.
Without the ripples,
We would all be alone.
Simplicity.

Insatiable

Unbridled passion.
A taste for desire unquenched.
Wanting, needing, longing for.
Lust, yearning, a thirst.
Insatiable
Man: "My loins burn for your goodness.
Ache to be within your essence.
My innards throb for your heart
See me, feel me , want me, love me.
I may not be who you want,
But I am who I am.
Please, take all that I have,
And let it stir inside your life giver."
Insatiable
Woman: "My moisture drips with intensity.
Walls are thumping with the beat of my heart.
With forbearance, I seek thee injection,
And the warmth of your caress.
Yet there's an ultimate desire.
Hold me, protect me, want me, love me.
The vulva wants and needs like any organ.
But my mind reads beyond the hymens request."
Insatiable.
Dream in your mind, that moment.
Let your wetness and hardness take control.
Place your fantasies on automatic pilot.
Let love be distant but,
At this time, passion has the rule.
Insatiable.

A Distant Shadow.

First of all, I pray that you get all you seek.
I hope your day is filled with all the joy and
happiness you deserve.
May your dreams and goals begin their
manifestation to your peak.
And may your heart stay tender, appreciated and
well served.
But let me tell you what I see.
In your eyes, I see all the tenderness and wonder
their beauty posses.
In your eyes, I see all the passion and love that's in
you.
I see in your eyes goodness and the purity that you
confess.
Also a heart that is as pure as gold too.
Yet I only have a short moment to gaze into this
gorgeous window,
I still and will remain a distant shadow.
In your smile, I see the glow of all the expectations
that you want
That precious joy and wonderful love that awaits
the receiver.
In your smile I see the sun and life through its
devious taunt
But I still have hope in what lies in it for the true
believer.
Even thought I revel in the briefness of this window
I still and will remain a distant shadow.

My World   K. Charles Latimer

In your beautiful face, there holds the weakness of
who I am.
However your thoughts are with another.
In your face, I conceit to that, so you see me as a
sham.
And I seem to fall prey to being just another
brother.
I hope that some day I will get out of that window,
But for now I still and will remain a distant shadow.
From day one that I saw you, you fascinated me to
no end.
But I have realized that you don't see me as I do
you.
And that all we maybe to each other are just
friends.
So I hope that we will stay in this way too
My dear, I wish not to read into my hope or any
factious window.
Maybe I'll just have to be satisfied with being your
distant shadow.

Is It Love?

Does lust confuse your mind?
Are your loins controlling your heart?
Do the hormones lead you astray?
Or is it simply that your private parts make you un-
smart.
Is it loneliness that guides your feelings?
Does an empty bed make you afraid?
An echo in the house, with no response.
Then you blame yourself for what you've made.
Is it really love?
Being by yourself, is not a bad thing.
Solitude has its' own pleasure.
Take this time to gather your thoughts.
Mental peace holds its' own treasure.
So think carefully whether your heart is warm.
Consider yourself when those palpitations beat.
You deserve someone who's worthy of your
goodness.
Not to just abide at another's feet.
Is it love?
Or is it about security?
Is the paper worth your pride and dignity?
Sure, money goes a long way.
You must think if this is your priority.
So, where lies your security?
I've learned that love is about me.
Yet it still guides me by the wayside.

My World   K. Charles Latimer

I lead, I bleed, I concede and I'm freed.
But my heart still seems to hide.
Is it love?
Is it truly love.....I wonder.

Believe in the Best

Love is great to give and to get.
It softens our hearts and soothes our minds.
And opens us up to the wonders of life.
Allowing us to feel sympathy for all mankind.
But there's another emotion just as strong.
It's like closing a door, with no worries of the rest.
My love for you, no one can compare.
However, for you and I, I only believe in the best.
If the world shatters your dreams,
Like It has a tendency to do.
Know that my belief in you excels all things.
No matter where, how or what you go thru.
With you, I have a strength yet unseen.
Let me lift you up, to help you bare the load.
My shoulders are built for the weight.
I promise, I won't scold, fold or explode.
Because there's another emotion just as strong.
It's like closing a door, with no worries of the rest.
My love for you, no one can compare.
However, for you and I, I only believe in the best.
Let life deal us all the worst hands that it may.
Together we will bare it, like a scaffold.
No path to crooked, nor a road to rough.
As we walk this course, all the way. your hand I'll
hold.
From the start, you were always in my heart.
Till today that has not, and will never, change.

My World   K. Charles Latimer

Because, I will be there for you, no matter what.
And that promise has no limit or range.
For there's another emotion just as strong.
It's like closing a door, with no worries of the rest.
My love for you, no one can compare.
However, for you and I, I only believe the best

Fresh Laundry

Is it me or has my perception of love changed?
I'm a few years passed a semi-century
And love has become like a dryer sheet.
It still smells sweet, yet we can vaguely see through
it.
Not seeing all the things we need to see.
Only the wisdom that is revealed to us
Even though the moisture of its inhabitance soften
it
The dry heat of pain, stiffens it, allowing us to see
better through it
I only hope and pray that mine left an air of sweet
remembrance
Yet I know there's mustiness in my garments
Because I let them sit in the closet too long
I've added Fa'Breeze but the odor was too pungent
I also put in dryer balls yet the heat was too much
They just melted and made a mess out of
everything
Maybe I should try.....but wait,
Note to oneself....., wash clothes first.

Pause A Moment

Lay the daily bustles down.
Put at ease, your righteous tensions.
Allow the heart to flutter at a sporadic rate.
From solar birth to lunar apex is not enough time.
There's a warming breeze to this moment,
Hugging us deep inside.
But pain is the bandleader that conducts our
rhythmic pulse.
With the winds of loneliness just a breath away.
Pause a moment.
Enjoy the hurt.
Submerge your all in the glow.
Cause both step together on this day.
My minds telling me no,
And my heart is screaming 'Hell no',
Yet love rules these hours,
As the glory of unity fills the soul.
Pause a moment.
Hear the twang of the bow.
The arrow has hit its spot with intended effect.
First, a sharp pain as it pierces.
Throbbing like a toothache.
Then, intoxicating you with fictitious love,
As you believe in the warmth you feel.
Again, both hold a simultaneous existence.
Also, striking an emotional consistence.
They row in the same boat of torment,
So take time to pause a moment.

Chapter Five

With all the negativity in our lives, what do we have to look forward to? Our jobs, don't appreciate us, don't pay us enough or don't utilize our talents the way they should. Then, like always, we get frustrated and wonder whether we should even go in to work on that day. As we lay in our beds we contemplate this, all the while knowing that we have to get up and go in. We have kids and family that depend on us to do these 7 or 8 hours of torture. So we get up, get dressed and go to a place that we despise, in order to take care of our love ones. This is not a life giving or taking thing but it is a priority, a must do to maintain a lifestyle that you and your people are accustomed to.

Your love life is dismal and discouraging, but we go out to seek and hope that we find that right person to share, add or make our lives happy. Most of the time, we come up short and fall for something or someone that is really not what we wanted. Then 3, 4 or 5 years pass by, where you can't put up with it anymore but you try to stay. Maybe for the kids' sake, because they have gotten use to them or you just don't want to go back out there looking again. Loneliness is indeed painful state that none of us want to be in and we fight hard not to be here. However, we settle for stuff so that we won't have to be in that state. I mean, who don't want the love of their lives? Who don't want the man or woman of their dreams? Yet our search goes unfulfilled and we end up crying at night from being alone or from regret.

We also go through the mind boggling thought of, 'what is my purpose in life.' None of us know for sure but we want a purpose. We want to have an idea of what that purpose is. Maybe even, what our direction in life and what we should be doing. I've had that thought and still have that enter my mind to this very day. Being 55, I still don't have an answer to that but I do say, to me and to others; "Just keep living and your purpose will come to you." Whether you are 25, 55, 75 or 95, your reason to be, will show itself. Be patient, take your time and just keep moving and it will become evident to you.

This is why this chapter is dedicated to positivity. With the former troubles that I spoke of, we must stay positive or why even live. Without something to live for, we would have no reason to breath another breathe. But, the thing about it is that we do have a reason. We do have a purpose and a means to live. That reason is simply us, we as an individual, are the reason. Let these poems remind you of these reasons and your purpose. I pray that

My World   K. Charles Latimer

these poems will give you a desire to say; "I will move on for another day." Let these poems motivate you for another hour, day or week because you are worth it. The world is worth you and what you have to give. Don't short me and don't short yourself. Read and gain strength.

Shoes That Fit.

I was in need of a new pair of shoes.
So after a good night sleep, I awoke refreshed.
Flip the butta jacks and poured on some Auntie J's.
Did the hot shower then splashed on some Armani
Gio.
I dressed to impress with my Van's on.
Topped my head in my best fedora.
Blessed my wrist in a black Movado.
Shaded my eyes, now I was ready to go.
As I entered my favorite shop,
All the shoes where beautiful.
Black, white, brown and yellow.
The selection was bountiful.
Every fantasy of shape and sizes were there.
My eyes were wide as I sought to choose.
I've made this mistake many of times.
So I must pick wisely or again I'd loose.
Suddenly, a pretty brown one caught my eye.
From afar, I felt the soul, warm and inviting.
I approached, engaged, hoping for a try.
I spent hours, spitting out sizes.
Then finally, slipping my foot in.
It takes months of adjustment, you to it and it to
you.
Please let these fit, cause I don't want to shop
again.
It's hard to find shoes that fit.
And with each wrong pair, makes you wanna quit.

Breeze

Blow.....as only you can.
You divide the chaff and whey.
Please......let the good settle.
As the bad keeps me interested.
Separate also, the happy and sad.
Along with the love and hate.
Can you keep one from affecting the other?
Like you did with the chaff and whey.
Breeze.
Or does a taste of one need to be in the other?
Maybe this was the intended purpose.
Cause one weighs heavier than its counterpart.
But that depends on the individual.
If the heart lays heavy with hate and bad,
Then that what will settle in the body.
However, good and love can still overcome.
If the mind continue to let those winds blow.
Breeze.

Solo Espera
(Just Wait)

Fast pace make an empty place
I know that the early bird catches the worm
But if you move to fast, your blessing will pass
And you will miss out on life
Take time to appreciate what is before you
Smell the flowers that are in your life
The little things keep us alive
But we tend to drive pass the signs
Solo espera
They seem to be that one
And your hopes are very high
Hearts warm to the excitement
Loins explode with vigor
And in the morning we wonder
What the fuck did we do
Who the hell is lying beside us
Too late, the deed is done
Solo espera

Your Ring

This ceremony was without fanfare and without
grandeur.
No reception was prepared with the absence of a
cake to cut.
The revelry of a bridal shower or bachelor's party
was unnecessary.
This moment was meant for more than the
accolades of spectators.
A union whose deeper purpose is more powerful
than the mind can phantom.
Embedded, spirit feeded and un-debted for I am in
He and He is in me.
Love that has been promised forever but tell me
did you forget your Ring?
We were made and created with the hopes of our
greatness.
And even the very air that we breathe was only
borrowed not gave.
Our placement on the chain was not earned
neither was it gained.
But this is an element of propitious beliefs from our
spousal expectations.
Our instructions were to oversee, name, and have
commission over all,

My World   K. Charles Latimer

With the bestowment of prosperity, eternal life,
and victory in every battle.
Our only requirement is to commit, confess,
believe and have faith.
It's a precious and vital union that was made, but
did you forget your Ring?
Blood was spilled for you, lashes were taken for
you, and nails were driven.
Spit upon for you, ridiculed for you and a life that
was sacrificed for you.
Every disease conquered, every weakness lifted,
and every evil abolished.
All the promises of life and existence are laid
delicately before us.
Are we too fickle, too arrogant and too stiff-neck to
marry our be trolled?
We wake because, we move because, we speak
because, and we live because.   He said; "Seek and
ye shall find," and "Ask and it shall be given."
His love, proposal and grace are rejected, again, did
you forget you Ring?
Our relationship, with Him, is inevitable, eminent
and forborne.
Yet we discard Him and ignored Him like a woman
that's scorned.
He has no intentions to harm or hinder our life, will
or way.

My World   K. Charles Latimer

His motive is to love, and to give from His heart but
not supersede our will.
This engagement we have was sealed by His blood,
breath, and His promise.
However it has to be agreed upon, by you, and
sealed with your very heart.
It has to be committed in His spirit and willing to be
used by His way.
You have to proclaim proud and loud that you're
His and to wear your Ring.
A ring that was given at our inception, and quickly
stained by deception.
It was presented, with all His glory and love, in the
essence of the first man.
However a thief, a liar and a destroyer,
unfortunately, was his best man.
So because of His intense desire and love, for the
bride of His choice.
This glorious ring was re-presented within the
fashion of the First Son.
There lingered no air of animosity, not even a
residual hint of despair.
Even though He was painfully rejected, fatal
attraction was not there.
Again the proposal is offered but where is your
Ring?

My World   K. Charles Latimer

Dearly beloved, we are gathered here with the
witness of all mankind.
To re-join and re-establish the union of the re-
essences of your essence.
And those in attendance, whom are, the bride,
groom and those in heaven.
Let them all agree to commit, honor and love one
another for all eternity.
Will those, in heaven, that bear witness attest and
apply to the same?
We know who detest this re-union so there is no
need for him to stand.
Do you, Lord, promise to love, cherish and commit?
"I do"
And do you, promise the Lord, to love, cherish and
commit? "I do"
So by the power invested in me, but wait, where is
your Ring?

YOU'VE WON !

Life deals many hands to us and we have to play
them to our best.
With each hand, we get two cards upfront and five
for all to play.
And like the game, we should Hold'em to see what
is laid.
In your hand you hold two deuces.
Four cards are laid out with a King and Queen
staring at you.
You are sure that the other players carry a better
hand, but you stay.
The last card is laid. A deuce, but you are still
skeptical.
But by faith you go all in, and surprisingly you hold
the best.
You've Won !!!
You have gone to college and earned your degree.
Applied for jobs in your field, with confidence.
With each card that's laid someone else gets the
better hand.
Frustration makes you want to throw it in.
You feel like you can't win, yet you wait on the last
card.
A full house beats three of a kind all day.
You've Won !

My World   K. Charles Latimer

For ten years you have worked on your job.
Put in over time, came in when needed and gave
110% each day.
You have shown the qualities for advancement and
your boss has seen it.
But four times you have been over looked for
promotion.
Irritated, you believe why should you try or keep
putting forth the effort.
With one last breath you go all in, you put in your
last and toss all forward.
Now you're the boss of those that passed you.
You've Won !
Those you love seem to leave you much too early.
It's like Death has taken residence in your life.
Misery and pain seems to cover you with no sight
of light.
Disappointment and unfulfilled goals has your
focus.
Yet throughout life you somehow hold on and hold
out.
You have continued to go on, go through and go
forth.
Afraid to see the next day but you rise up to see it.
The prince of momento mori wants you to sleep
and stay.
But as the last card is laid you open your eyes and
rise.
Just by that act, by that defiant move or
unconscious response.
You've Won !

My Purpose

Ask for what you want, put in your order.
Believe and know that you already have it today.
In your mind, receive and feel like you have it now.
Always expect the best in life and I promise, you
may.
Your purpose is what you say it is.
Your goals are what you stand on, for you've won.
Your mind is focused on what you want.
Forget the ounce and expect the ton,
Change your mindset and thoughts.
Visualize your success, til it burns in your gut.
Be grateful for what you have, for you've come a
long way.
Don't worry about how it will happen.
Just know it will happen, and on that path you
should stay.
There's a law of attraction, that you must consider.
The good that's around you,
With a positive mind, that you will attract.
But, like a magnet, negativity will too.
So, focus on the good and all around you will be so.
Think abundance and so shall you be.
Picture your happiness, in your mind.
And your physical eyes will see.
Your purpose, is what you say it is.
Your goals are what you stand on, for you've
won.
Your mind is focused on what you want.
Forget the ounce and expect the ton.

Is There A Reason?

The cares of the morning dew cleans yet another
day.
Still the filth of the past holds your mind at bay.
Even with the soothing rise and warmth of the sun,
That should give you all hope and vision.
The heaviness of your earthly pathos still gags and
bounds your life.
We wonder what, when and why or is there a
reason at all for our dilemma.
There's the rhythmic tune and the fleeting
commencement sounds,
Of a bright and shinning new beginning.
Giving rose-colored beliefs of what's to come your
way.
But the depravity of the world opens the door to
man kinds treason.
So you think; "Is there a reason?"
As the day goes by the sun sets, the grind is over
and the workday has passed.
You have little to believe in yet you keep moving
on.
You have no more than before but you still keep
going strong.
Time goes by and you see many seasons,
Still you wonder; "Is there a reason?"

My World   K. Charles Latimer

The breath of life has been giving to you.
The gift of knowledge you have been blessed with
too.
The ability of choice is yours as well.
Doing right or wrong is yours to sell.
Doing what's right feed the seed of good things.
Yet sometimes we don't see the gifts it brings.
However doing wrong only your gut knows the
reason.
And with that wrong, you still say; "Is there a
reason?"

By The Way...

We have looked at your rental history and see your
residence at several places.
Your payment history is not great but it's
consistent.
Here we have a strict residence policy with firm
rules that we must apply by.
And by the way, we will not be able to grant your
request for residency.
Your application is impressive and you have a great
deal of experience.
I am also pleased with your appearance and your
professionalism.
Even the salary, that you request, is within a
reasonable amount we can pay.
However, by the way, we are not looking for
someone of your stature right now.
I've went over your credit application with my
credit manager and sales manager.
We all agree that you would be a prime candidate
for our credit building program.
Even though the model of car you chose is a fine
vehicle and within your budget.
Unfortunately, by the way, we can't finance you at
this time.

My World   K. Charles Latimer

We have done several cat scans and other tests
and the cat scans looked fine.
Your overall health is something we can be
confident in and work on.
There are concerns in the other tests that may not
be very positive.
But, by the way, you have cancerous tumor and it's
malignant.
Every trouble in the world has come upon you and
you feel heavy laden.
No one seems to give you a break or relay any good
news to you.
But you must know that Christ died on the cross for
your troubles and sickness.
And, by the way, you have victory over all things
through His name.

IT TAKES ONLY ONE MAN.

By the grace of our Eternal Creator a change must
always take place.
The pride of mankind goes into automatic defense
mode,
As our fleshly mind revert back to adolescent
tantrums.
Not considering the greater good of all living
things,
Or even the advancement of the human race.
To see a brighter picture, it takes only one man
Our selfish tendencies always get in the way
We seem to cut our nose off to spite our faces
Lest someone else gets more
To change that, it takes only one man
Hate is a burden that is hard to carry
Yet some of us tote it out of fear
Ignorance also plays a factor, as you carry it
Allowing the blinders to keep you in darkness
Love can soothe those wombs and it takes only one
man
Since the beginning of time a change has come by
just the swipe of His hand.
From Genesis, the tale of our creation,
To Revelation, a story that manifest our salvation.
His greatest changes always start with just one
man.

I'll Sleep Well

Hate on me.
Talk about me.
Judge my character.
Spit my name in the streets.
I'll sleep well.
I worry not,
What you think of me.
I worry no,
How you talk about me.
I'll sleep well.
The weight is on you.
The stress you bear.
You tried to discourage me.
But God, freed me from it.
I'll sleep well.
So do what you feel.
Maybe, it makes you feel better.
I turn my back to your swell,
Because, trust me,
I'll sleep well.

His Presence.

Who hasn't read of, or have not been made aware?
Who out there has never felt the power of a room
filling up,
Being on your knees, in your closet, as you pray.
Even though you are alone and there is no one
there?
Who, I wonder, who has not felt it as you go to and
fro,
Something giving you an insight, a warning or, a gut
feeling
That makes you stop, turn around and go back or
pause,
Because you believe this is not what you should do
or the way to go.
Who, I feel sorry for you, but who has not been
covered at church,
With that invisible and indescribable, blanket of
warmth and goodness.
Which causes you to shed tear of joy, shout like
never before,
As you find what you've been missing and
relinquish your search.
Please, please, please don't tell me but I pray to
God it's not you.
It's not you who missed out on His guiding hand.

My World   K. Charles Latimer

Waiting to encourage and ready to see you
through.
For the love of God, please tell me this is not you.
It's not you, whom He saved when you couldn't
even save yourself,
Yet you put His loving kindness away on a shelf.
Tangled up in a web of worldly troubles,
And your only worry and concern is for yourself.
But if it is you, let me give you a golden nugget to
live by.
It only three words of wisdom, not by size but by
substance,
That can change your life forever and they are;
Seek His Presence.

Fire and Ice

During the savages of life, we all play a game with
fire and ice.
Let he whom desire life shed the fickle clothe of
the flesh.
And cover thy self with the vestiges of the
soothing, icy blue sky.
Daily we fight a battle between the chill of ice and
the rage of fire.
Yet, the fight is unbalanced, because the fire is
vigorously fed each day the eyes are open.
Then ice comes along to shock us awake and will to
cool the burn, if sought.
But the Devil's door stay's temptingly open with a
fire that attracts us like moths.
And just as the moth, our destruction is inevitable.
However, we run from the truth, the peace and the
coolness of Shaddai, with fear.
One day we will all learn from the burn and firmly
turn to the other side of the pillow.
Once we have learned to stay away from the may
lay, then at the gate, we have truly paid our fair.
But why do we find comfort in the burning flames
of the fire?
This is truly a question only the individual can really
answer.

My World   K. Charles Latimer

Search the heart and the mind, but they are also
part of the flesh.
Maybe that's why the feel the pain of the burn
more the anything.
Solution, change the inner parts of the heart and
mind.
By seeking the cool, refreshing waters of
everlasting life.
However, most people have a fear of being cold
then being hot, think for a moment.

DO I LOSE?

I always wonder what lovebirds feel when they are
together.
Do they actually express love for one another?
Or is that just the imagination of man kinds quest
for an emotional connection.
I imagine that birds have their way of showing their
affection.
Probably more real and true then we as being the
dominate creatures.
But most animals show their true intentions
without the element of deceit.
To them love is an unconditional factor that needs
no embellishment.
But we use it as a weapon to entice, control and
influence.
So do we really live up to the expectations that the
creator gave us?
We tend to fall short of the basic principles of
animalistic existence.
Simply put, we lose.
Our minds and hearts rationalize the levels of why
or why not.
Our guts and emotions supersede what our natural
instincts employ.

My World   K. Charles Latimer

Greater are our intellect and ability to solve
problems.
We have the brain power to piece together a
simple puzzle.
The cognitive fortitude to envision what can or
should be.
We possess the imagination to invent and create all
manner of tangibility.
The world is full of the creature comforts that our
minds have aspired.
Yet the truth of love and the simple dedication of it
seems to escape us.
However the animal kingdom finds a way to
dedicate, and love with truth.
They have an understanding, between them, that
makes our superiority void.
So the question remains, as humans, do we lose.
We fight, avoid, cover up and make excuses for the
truth of love.

BY THE WAY THE WIND GOES.

As a crisp autumn wind blows,
It effects all in its path.
The origin or destination, no one really knows,
Yet lays the theories of those we trust to do the
math.
Meanwhile, as we conjure, a leaf flows.
Not by its own will, or decision,
It is whipped and pulled as it goes.
As it is directed by the winds precision,
Does this leaf have a choice of the road that it
takes?
Which way it should go or which move to make?
Mindlessly driven by the winds tow,
Controlled and guided by the way the wind goes.
Christ said, on the boat, as the waters raged near,
"Ye of little faith," have no fear.
It wasn't the waters, as He stood, that He
demanded,
But the wind He told: "Be still," that he
commanded.
Like the waters, the leaf has no option but to go
where it is sent.
Even though its true Maker knows where it is
meant.
The end of this journey, to the leaf, the Master,
does not show.

My World   K. Charles Latimer

It can only trust in the wings by the way the wind
goes.
But we, as humans, think we have no right wind to
guide us.
We tend to get caught up in the worldly winds that
surround us.
We seem to fall prey by the waters at bay, the
routes that say, or the directions that lay,
When, like the waters in the Bible, there is a source
and we have a choice.
And, unlike the leaf, we have a mind to select a
course, of course.
But like the leaf, we only ride on the winds that
surround us, and at the end that's where we will
land.
Our true hopes and beliefs are the cornerstone on
where we stand.
The leaf has no option, to which it flows,
But, as humans, we can control by the way the
wind goes.

Chapter Six

We all have a talent that we strive to bring forth and mine is writing. Whatever yours is, do it, pursue it and thrive at it. I have always loved writing, whether it's poems, books or articles, I just love to write, to put my thoughts on paper and to make my ideas known. I believe that my writings will live long after I'm gone, they will be my heritage, my legacy, my children. Creativity is a long aspired discipline that many have tried to display through paintings, writings or whatever they feel. No one can or should diminish what you have to offer, what your mind sees and what your thoughts create. Don't worry or concern yourself whether others get it, see it or understand it, just do what you do and feel what you feel.

My thoughts are, sometimes, beyond what most people feel or think but I will continue to write, to put my thoughts on paper, whether anyone gets it, believes it or even understands it. Because I'm sure that no one can see into my mind, my thoughts or my imagination. I have always had a vivid

My World   K. Charles Latimer

imagination, since I was young, and I'm grateful for that, because it has lead me to this point.

What is it that you feel you have that no one else can display? What does your mind envelope that no one else has to offer? You have it, your mind has imagined it and your fantasies has believed it. Why must we limit ourselves to what others think is acceptable? What makes us think that we have to be bound by whatever others believe we should adhere to?

We are not that. We are not tied to that. We are a culture that aspires, vision and strives for more. We believe more, we look beyond what anyone can imagine. This is why creativity is so important to our society and why it is vital to us as a people. I hope that these poems move, stir, lift and help you grow, as a person. My books, poems and articles are meant to do that.

Utopia

I know joy is a level of thought.
And what you enjoy is an element of the present.
Passion brings this into focus
However, the truth of joy is a dessert.
If my bed is cold, how do I see joy?
But I must grind it out for the best.
And make kool ade out of lemonade.
Give the pain to yesterday,
Just let life be a constant fade.
I love my being and all it contains,
What He has given me, I don't deserve.
Take care of me, oh Lord,
Because all I can do is serve.
Love just simply runs from me,
Or is it that I run from it.
Utopia is something that can't feel
Or is it something I won't obtain.
I just want to love someone who loves me.
Why does this have to be such a strain.
Lay me down, oh Lord, and give me release.
Or give me someone that loves me for who I am.
Let me know that Utopia is not a fantasy.
But something that will not cease.
Utopia, what the hell is that,
I can't even dream or phantom that joy.
Yet, the thought of it stays in my mind.
How do I obtain the Utopia of love.

Let alone to enjoy.
Love scares me and how do I top that,
Maybe Utopia is way beyond my mind frame.
Several times I gave it a try,
I guess I didn't have the game.

The Call

(*ring ring, ring ring, ring ring.*)
Hello.
Hi. How are you?
Fine. Who is this?
I'm someone who can help you.
How?
I can benefit you beyond your means.
In what way?
Do you remember that incident with your boss today?
Yes, how do you know about that?
I was there.
Where were you? Who is this?
Do you remember the argument with your father?
Yes, how do you know about that?
Because, I am always with you.
This is not funny. Who are you?
I am someone you cannot see but I am always there.
Me and my father talked in private so how could you have been there?
Did he not disagree with your choice of your job change?
Yea, so how do you know that? The only one that could have known that must been there but my father and I were alone.
But I was there.

My World   K. Charles Latimer

I'm hanging up because I think you are full of crap.
*Don't hang up because you are going to need my
help.*
I don't need no help from someone I don't know.
*You do not know me but you do. You think I do not
know you but I have always known you.*
Enough games. Who is this?
*I am what is in you but you fail to see. I am your
best decision but you are too stubborn to hear me.*
Who is this, the Lord?
*I am not He but I am a part of Him, which is you. I
am your conscience and your right decision. I am
what is good for you, yet you do not know it. I am
the goodness, kindness and truth that lies in you
but you cannot see. I am that conversation that you
have within yourself that you do not listen too, and
regret later. You have refused to listen to me before
and things have turned out bad for you. So I have
only one question. Can you hear Me now? Will you
pay attention to yourself or your inner self, or is it
too late? Your goodness lies within yourself but will
you take the time to listen to it? Before you can
hear your outer being, you have to hear your inner
being which part of the Holy Spirit that is in you. So
if you do not hear that then how can you hear Him?*

Ripples of the Crowd.

Have you heard the roar of the crowd?
The cheers of the many.
The influence from the populous.
Does this not weight heavy on you?
To allow the harrows of your thoughts,
Change the rivers that flow.
Release yourself from the umbilical waters of the
past.
Restrain the ravenous leanings by the hounds of
hell.
Engulf yourself in the beatitudes of generations
before.
And give in to the proprieties of the heart.
Give effort to yield to the purity of humanity.
Our innards are not born to animosity and fear.
Nor is it derived from hatred and greed.
That is our outer shell we fall prey to.
We are initially made of kindness and goodness.
Our essence is comprised with respect and love.
Yet the gaggle tweaks our insecurities leading us
astray.
Lo those who beckon the call of the many.
Lo those who seek council from the despaired.
However raise yourself beyond the depths of
worldly duplicities.
Reach out for your embedded coup de maître.
Let the roots of kindness infuse the inert elements
of agape.
For he whom swims in the ripples of many,
Is often drowned by the lack of belief in his self.

Close Sez Me!

What shall you yield when the gates are close?
Only those whom assume the interior shall have
hopes to decorate it.
Yet some approach the entrance without the code.
And some try when there are no tickets to be sold.
The heart is the gate and love is the ticket.
You may invest in the ticket of love,
Still the heart will not allow.
It's garbage, it's trash, it's outdated and it's
worthless.
When the heart is shut down then what can you
achieve?
We all have been hurt in our hearts and mind,
Then what do we perceive.
But if we don't spend time, know the crime and
rewind,
We will never know the fine.
Because it take time to get into the gates of the
heart and many have to wait.
Yet still, some gates remain close never to be open
by man.
This was the individuals' choice and only God can
solve it.
But understand that these gates were not closed as
a child.
They were only locked by the growth of humanity.

My World   K. Charles Latimer

And humanity can't unlock these gate only make
them fortified.
How can they if they don't even possess the key?
However God knows the code and only He can see.
The heart is our foundation and all will make a
plea.
Yet we all need to realize that only God has the
key.

For I Am

I script a language of the imagination.
An emotional expression in a rhythmic fashion.
An artistic written display of thoughts.
Wrapped into a passionate cushion.
Who am I?
For I am the poet.
I command, snuggly between appendages, a tool, a
weapon.
An endless instrument limited only by the
imagination.
That can be as useful as need be.
Or lay futile, in stagnation.
Who am I?
For I am the poet.
I blend together, life's inversions.
Into a more palatable mix that one may consume.
Even though, the taste maybe bitter,
My style gives you reason to subsume.
Who am I?
For I am the poet.
I spew forth, with a writing instrument,
Fanatic fantasies, born from the heart.
And display them with grace.
To pluck the strings of your inner heart.

My World   K. Charles Latimer

Who am I?
For I am the poet.
I am the director of an ever changing veintiseis
chorus,
That can produce a sweetness of sound,
To astound, confound and expound,
All that you know to be sound.
Who am I?
For I am the poet.
I create magical moments where pen and paper
engage in copula.
Whereas the mind is the ruptured condom.
That avows the birth of heirs.
As time constricts conception to the quondam.
Who am I?
For I am the poet.

WATCH !

This is not a moment or method to hypnotize.
This is not a mind conducing or inducing faction to
put you under a trance.
No, think what you want to think.
Let your mind go where you want it to go.
Don't concentrate on the watch,
Let the movement of the watch take you to a place
where you are at peace.
Let your surroundings be your guide.
Let all around you, teach you, train you, enlighten
you.
But keep your eye on the watch.
Allow your ears to listen to the tick, tick, tock.
Because your concentration comes from the sound.
And your eyes are just a filter of the colors you see.
Sight can fool you, for it's based on interpretation.
Tick tock, tick tock, hear the rhythm of the watch.
If you let all thoughts go, your mind will show you
something new.
Let that newness change your life, if you want it to.
Feel alive, feel awake, feel reborn.
Your birth pains are in your sight, but you emerge
between the tick and tock.
Listen to that rhythm and be made anew.

Fantasia

Fantasia is where the seeds of the imaginations
lives and grows.
Here, the wonders of dreams come together,
To the pleasure of the dreamer.
And as I marry pen to paper, in vivid colors of hope,
This is just a sample of the images that's in my
mental show.
As the light glimmers from my laptop,
I desire that the images in my mind would come to
life.
Like the ambitions of Gepetto,
Praying breathe into the vision before him.
I too await and yearn, because my breathing has
stopped.
Captivated by my thoughts that are frozen in their
place.
I'm eager to reveal the fantasies that roam in the
subconscious.
Feeling the warmth of my imagination,
Yet statured by the coldness of the heart.
My fingers trace the angelic symmetry of an image
in space.
Deeper I dwell into that stimulating fantasia,

My World   K. Charles Latimer

Closing my eyes and hoping to bring that image
into script.
My fingers, tenderly, stroke the keys,
Trying to display the passion of my thoughts.
I can feel my whole body embrace the words I
write.
My mind flips, my heart skips and my soul trips.
Then reality jars me from my fantasia,
Cutting me short from my written display of
emotion.
Frustration obtrudes my peace of mind.
However, the echoes of my thoughts,
Remain in my mental reverberation.
Leaving a soothing blueprint for another day.

Chapter Seven

Here's the problem y'all, Black people don't want nothing that you don't already have. We have been here, fought, died, built and have help established this country, just as much, if not more so, then any other culture. Why do we have to fight for what we have earned, what we have shed blood for and what we have given life for? You fought against the British, to gain freedom, against the Germans, for tyranny, but when we, as black people fight, we are labeled as un-American, unpatriotic and haters of the country.

Why are we the most hated culture in the world? Why does every race seem to hate us and think we are thugs, criminals or bad people? We, as a culture, has done no more than the Italians, the Scots, the Indians, the Asians but all these cultures hate us and are scared of us.

Why, because the TV, the media and all that you see of us is bad. Your mind has been implemented to think that we are bad people. Your ideas of us have been triggered to be leery of us. When we come around, you have an automatic response to be fearful of us and I still trying to figure out why?

My World   K. Charles Latimer

The KKK has been terrorizing black people for centuries. The Italian mob has been wreaking havoc for decades. The Asians mafia has been killing Americans for a long while. But back in the 40s, 50s and 60s, when all this was going on, black people just wanted you to leave us alone, but you wouldn't. Black Panthers tried to give you the message, Malcolm tried to give you the message, and Martin tried to be one with you and you still didn't want to play nice. Marcus asked that you leave us alone, Emmitt just wanted to get alone but a white girl said he did something that he didn't do, so you killed him. Black Wall Street just wanted to be, but you feared that so you found a reason to destroy that. Many more black people just tried to blend and get along with you but you didn't want that. What do you expect us to do? How do you expect us to react?

We've tried, but you've denied. We've put forth the effort but you have slapped our hand back every time. We've made a move to get along but you have refused our efforts. So what do we do now? We must take what you have refused to give us. We must take the rights that you have tried so hard to deny us. We must find and claim our culture that you have hid from us for so long. We are the originals, we are the first born, we are the beginning and you know that but you try to hid that because you thought we would never see the truth. Now that some of us are seeing the real, you are scared. Obama was not a freak of nature, it was

My World   K. Charles Latimer

inevitable. It is just a peek into the future of what will happen in the US. Many will fight this, many will protest this but it will be what it will be. White people, you are no longer the majority, in this country, you are the minority. Live with it, deal with it and just accept it. These next couple of poems are just a look into what we, as black people, deal with on a daily bases and what we feel everyday.

The Awakening.......

There's an enlightenment shining on the world, as
we know it.
The glow of truth that has long been shunned.
I will cause pain for some, hate and fear for others.
But The Awakening of my people, has begun.
The history, of a people, that they hoped we've
forgotten.
With the true roots of our race,
And the contributions we've done.
However, true light will shine through white
washed shit.
Now, The Awakening of my people had begun.
With the 12 tribes of Israel, that we derived from,
To the real Jewish nation, in which we come.
For centuries, this lie has been laid for the benefit
of some,
Finally, The Awakening of my people has begun.
Now, the ultimate deceit of Christ has come to
light.
While the truth begins to shine, to the chagrin of
some,
How can a man, born from a dark ancestry, still be
white?
Again, The Awakening of my people has begun.

My World   K. Charles Latimer

During the 50s, 60s and 70s, our race begin to see.
The strength of our origin and lies started to flee.
In the 80s and 90s, with our dukes up, we swung.
Thank God, The Awakening of my people is in full
strung.
Obama's in office and some think we should rest,
That just brought out the truth of some people's
real ugliness.
We've got a thousand pounds, yet we strive for a
ton.
It's The Awakening of my people, it's time for us to
have the gun.

Samson

Strenght
is
your
downfall.
Muscles,
Strong
big
and
Impressive,
Yet
Leaves you weak and empty.
I have not your specter,
Yet, I fight a disease
and every day,
my strength is greater
then yours.
For my fight is inside,
And yours is only with man.

READ THIS !!

Individuality is a grand concept of time, but read
this.
We are all some ones father, some ones mother,
some ones sister and some ones brother,
Living on this speck of dust in the universe.
As if we are the only existence in this vastness.
And to us we are, for no one lives here but us.
We are all we know and here we all glow,
To survive by the newness of each other's lives.
We take, we give. We die, we live. We work, we
play. We lie and we pray, upon this we thrive.
One family, one neighborhood, one state, one
country and one world, on this we exist.
So think for a moment, as you read this.
Take heed, for a minute, our creation while you
read this.
Big Bang and evolution is a song played by the
scientists' horns.
But I believe that we are greater than the excretion
from a monkeys loins.
However, we steal and we kill, yet justify it for
religious sake.
Giving weight to the theory that our ancestors are
primates.
Religion is an element used to divide us, the
separatists' tool,

My World   K. Charles Latimer

Spirituality means, we are one, which follows the
lines of Gods rules.
We all strive to see the glory of Gods brand new
day.
Fighting because of religion is simply not the way.
Others beliefs are for us to learn and gather
wisdom but not dismiss.
Put that in your pipe and smoke on it, as you read
this.
Let the splendor of love grow in your heart when
you read this.
Is love the unbridled and unconditional force that
drives you?
Or is it just a spitted word used to fool who?
The glory of real love should be with no weights or
measures.
To spread freely to all and not lock it up like a
treasure.
I agree, there's a love that you give to those whom
earned.
But the strength of love is shown by covering the
flames of hate that burns.
We are born from love, by love and with love,
some may see.
Others count themselves as a late night tryst or a
lustful epiphany.
To those whose hearts are heavy, hardened and
see no sign of bliss,
Know this, God loves you and that's all that
matters, as you read this.

My World   K. Charles Latimer

You don't look like me, or I, like you. Irrelevant, so
read this.
My color, you didn't understand but your excuse
was hate not fear.
Thought to be animals and insentient beings, made
ignorance shed a tear.
Killed by the billions, yes I said billions, and soon to
change that B to a Z.
For the children's, children's of those murdered,
will never be.
Let's not forget the Jewish, Indians and other
massacres on your plate.
Racism is an evil beast that still hasn't erased its
slate.
By now society should know better, yet it still lives
like a bug.
We should recognize it, eliminate it and not let it
crawl under the rug.
Yes, it is changing but I still see it every day, how
long must we exist.
Let's wake up from the dream and make it reality
to never again have to read this.

Incessant Whisper

Relish the warming caress of her embrace
She is soothing, yet her tongue tingles with a single
lick
Concede to her delicate kiss that can tease and
trick
Recreating sensations of the past and present, with
grace
Only fooling yourself, that you're able to cease her,
to touch her or to resist her grip
You're unwarned by the sight of her arrival
The gentle sounds of her soft spoken words are
primal
They chill like the placid blow of a lover breathe
that slips
Repulse, not her moves nor anger her to force
With a voice that can rip at you with voracity and
passion
Like the echoes of a thousand horses, you will hear
her
Pouring forth the howls of wolves but you know
her voice
So take comfort in the mellow songs of
reconciliation
Because, just like those of her kind, she will shift
and stir.

Natures Blend.

I'm the waterfall,

And I pour into your lake.

We blend together.

I drip in your walls,

And life has become a new.

Then we are now one.

With fear, we move on,

But in belief, we will stand.

So, let the pond be.

The lake loves the falls.

Truly, vise-versa, alike.

On this, the pond grows.

If the water slows,

There's no way the pond can grow.

Eventually, dries.

Audentes Fortuna Luvat

(Fortune favors the Bold)

Have you ever asked the question: "Why are we
Black?"
History, as it's written, tells us we are inferior.
Yet the truth has begun to come out.
Open eyes and minds know differ, we are superior.
Being black is not a load to bear.
Nor is it a levy against you.
Being black is a call to greatness.
For this is not given to the many, but the few.
Audentes fortuna luvat.
We have learned that being black is not the back of
the bus.
Neither is it not going where we choose.
America has slowly begun to figure this out.
With us, we win, without us, you lose.
So again, why are we black?
Because we are the epiphany of reality.
We are the beginning of existence and the end of
life.
Mother of life, was this color. Very few will deny.
Most black people know it, but others with strife.
Audentes fortuna luvat.
Contrary to your books facts.
The chosen Jews were black.
But many fight to dis-believe that.
They came from Africa, come on jack.
I love the hue in which I display.

My World   K. Charles Latimer

By my tone, tells you, I'm a unique breed.
I have been blessed by the creator.
Despite all your chains and ropes, I have long been freed.
Audentes fortuna luvat.
Which means, "fortune favors the bold."
So, why are we black, still a question in your mind.
We are meant to control, un-fold, to gain and re-hold,
For all that God gave, on this earth, was up to us to find.

Who Am I ?

Who am I?
I am only one in a billion wading in her maternal
waters.
The race is on.
The pace was strong.
And no matter what happens afterwards,
I was a winner before I was formed.
Then nine months later I surged,
I emerged, purged of the ungodliness of this world.
I was beautiful.
Blood dripped, but I was not cut.
Dying, yet I was not wounded.
I took my first breath of life,
Or should I say, I inhaled the air of death.
Maybe this is why we cry when we are born.
Who am I?
Now I am a bow-legged toddler who is taught how
to walk and talk.
Who is taught how to read, write, run and play.
But who is taught, unintentionally some may say,
To hate, to lie, to steal, to kill and other forms of
barbaric behavior.
But love we were not taught,
For this was the filmy cape we donned whence we
emerged.
As it was washed away, just like that, we took a
step back,
And from that moment on, the lesson of un-love
begin.

My World   K. Charles Latimer

But who am I?
Today I'm a man who carries in him the essence of,
Millions that were enslaved, battered, killed and
dismayed,
Yet I try, I sigh, I cry and ask why,
And they still have the nerve to say Hitler was the
bad guy.
So what does that make you good, huh?
No, you just know how to lie.
But what's sad is that the fore-mentioned
travesties,
Are still going on today.
Daily they stare, as if I have never been seen
before,
And follow me all around the store.
They clutch their purses tightly, all the while eyeing
me
They've been watching too much Menace to
Society.
So inside I scream, Oh Lord, help me get through
this day.
But with each day, as I wake and see the glory of
the sun,
I venture forward into this world eager to learn my
daily lesson,
On how to re-love again.
So who am I?
I am a winner.
But wait!
That's what I was in the beginning

Where Are We

I'd like to think that we are in our peace.
I'd like to believe we reside in our lasting place.
But with the hate that surrounds our existence,
We are no better than those that came before.
Yes, we desire, we want and we think.
That we are better, as time has gone by.
Yet, where are we really?
We war, we kill, we think that one is above the
other.
Why do we insist on being so hateful?
Why are we so determined to separate?
Love comes so damn easy.
So, where are we?
Brother against brother, father hating mother.
Sister despising sister, family detesting family.
When we die, apologies seems useless.
But for our satisfaction, we think it justifies.
Again, where are we?
Can we love the way we should,
With intelligence?
Why....Why..Why?
But ignorance leaves us where we are.

What More Can I Do?

What more can I do?
I have relinquished my children to the cruelty of
bondage.
I have bended a knee to your self- serving
superiority.
I have allowed you to separate me from my kin.
And I only watched as you murdered those I love.
What more can I do?
What more can I do.....
As you ignored your promise of 40 acres and a
mule.
As you gave me nothing to sustain myself.
As you cheated me from an honest way to farm.
And blocked any move I made to be free, even
though, you promised me.
What more can I do?
What more can I do...
You prevented me from learning and killed those
who tried to teach me.
Even though you treated worst then a dog and
expected me to abide.
Even though you beat me, hung me as a Saturday
night whim.
And then act as if I should just forget and move on.

My World   K. Charles Latimer

What more can I do?
What more can I do...
When you gave me the right to vote yet prevented
me to do so.
When you bar me from a simple water fountain.
When you banned me to the back of the bus.
Because Jim Crow was the hidden law of the land.
What more can I do?
What more can I do...
You tell me to buy a house but give me shitty loans.
You tell me to get a job but don't pay me what I
deserve.
You tell me to rely on justice but cops kill me and
jail me for minor crimes.
Yet, you ask me to trust you but you have given me
little reason to do so.
What more can I do?
This is what I can do
I will stand up and take what I should have.
I will refuse to let you treat me like a second class
citizen.
I will defend myself and my family from you by any
means necessary.
And I will learn all I can to get all I can.
I will do it and you can't and won't stop me.
That's what I can do.
And that's what I will do.

The Mess You Made.

The process is good, but those that run it, not so much. I feel the justice but I don't think that the justice feels me. I love America but does America love me? My skin doesn't fit your plan. Why? Because you have already leveled me to be less than you. Justice has no meaning to me. Equality has no meaning to me, because you make it so. However, you want me to believe that all things are equal, yet they are not and you show me that everyday of my existence. If we are equal, show me. Not by your words but by your actions.

Our minds can quickly make up pretty white sheets to cover up our beds, to which we will have to eventually lie in. Now, whether we are truly surprised what's there when we pull those sheets back, only the individual will know. Nevertheless, we will still have to, at some time, lay in what we hid underneath.

With that being said, what you do unto others, a fear will haunt you that they will do the same unto you. And what so ironic about when that time comes, you will actually wonder why these things are happening to you. If you stand in front of a fan and throw shit at the fan, how can you be surprised when the shit comes back on you.

A race of people brutalized, tortured and massacred to the brink of non-exsistence for centuries simply because it served your purpose.

My World   K. Charles Latimer

To be force into servitude, belittled and not
allowed to learn in order to better themselves,
because you believe that they were less than you
or unable to learn so that you could maintain your
self-proclaim superiority. Then when we got a
crumb from a steak that we should have had, you
put restrictions on how to eat the little piece that
we got. 40 acres and a mule, reneged. A chance to
farm the land and sell goods fairly, blocked and
cheated. A chance to build schools and teach our
children a better way, schools burned teachers
hanged.

Then you gave us a bigger piece of that steak,
the right to vote. As with the small piece, you put
restrictions on this as well. Making voting centers
out of reach. Giving ridiculous tests to pass before
you could vote, like guessing the number of
marbles in a bowl. Making us read and sign things
when you knew that a lot of us could not read or
write due to the restrictions you had placed on us
since being brought here.

Yet again, you dangle an even bigger piece of
that steak in front of us, the Civil Rights Act,
knowing that the Jim Crow laws, of the era, would
not make it easy to take advantage of. For you, it
was just a game, a Saturday night outing with the
boys. But for us it was our life our future and our
very existence. For you it was keeping the natural
order of things and maintains your delusional white
people's power. For us it was making our way in
this country, by any means necessary. It was

showing our children's that we are just as much American, if not more, than those that what to keep us oppressed. This was the true definition of a life and death situation.

Now, even the times that we live in today, you continue to dangle a piece of steak at us, as if we haven't learned that it comes with restrictions. Try to buy a house, either they don't give you the loan or give you the loan on a house that in a neighborhood where the property values don't increase or constantly decrease. Give you a job that below your skillset, pay you less then deserved or tell you that you are not qualified for the position. Example; Right to Hire. This gives states, if you didn't know, the right to hire whomever and not based on the best qualified. Also, the right to fire you for whatever reason they see fit and they do not even have to tell you what that reason was. And let's not forget the justice system. Cops can and will kill us without repercussions. Judges sentence us to jail time more often, with much more time to serve for petty crimes. This keeps our dreams of freedom at bay and put us into a system that like a revolving door. Because when we get out of jail, no one what to hire us so we go back to survival mode and end up right back in jail. I read were a black lady shot at a guy and got sentenced to 20 years but a white police woman killed a black guy and was sentenced to only 10 years. A white guy killed a police dog attacking him and got probation however, a black did the same and got

40 years.

So white people stop giving us a pieces of the steak that we should already have and then put it in a cage where we can't get to it without going through a bunch of tricks. Jews....reparations. Asians....reparations....Indians......reparations. So why is it wrong for black people to ask, request or demand reparations?

Our suffering was this countries doing so it's this countries responsibility to repair it, hence the word reparations. This is the mess in your bed and it's time to clean it up because if you don't, please don't cry when you have to lay in that bed.

Chapter Eight

The love we have for our family is greater than anything. We may get upset with our blood relatives but, when they're gone, we find out how much they were a part of us. Blood means just that, blood. It's not only what we share but who we are and where we come from. Some of the members of our family tree, we probably wouldn't have gotten along with but they are our heritage, our roots and without them, we would simply not be.

Being black, there is a safe assumption that my heritage came from the slave culture. However, there are many black people that came from freemen, where their ancestors had never been slaves, yet still, they came from Africa.

I'm pissed by the fact that, with most of black people here, we can't trace our ancestors back to the Motherland. They only go back to the late 1800s because no real records of slaves were kept. But you have these bullshit sites like Ancestry.com that really don't know crap about where you came from. They just fill a black persons head with what they think, not what they know. That's why they are so wide spread with their findings. They will give a black person five or six tribes in Africa, that they could have possible came from, yet they don't know for sure. So, solely, because of white people we don't know our true heritage, our real legacy and the royalty that our culture came from. I think that's by design because they are in fear of who we are. They are afraid to admit that we are the foundation of mankind, we are the beginning of humans and that when God made man, it was us. Even scarier to them is that Christ was a black man, where they base their, self-serving, superiority from. Also that the Egyptians Pharaohs and Queens were black people, but that truth is coming out in droves, making it hard for them to white wash history anymore.

For now, I'm proud of the little heritage that I know and I wish that I had spent more time with my elders, so that I could learn more about my lineage. From what I know, my mother was 1/4th Cherokee Indian, which made my grandma ½ Cherokee but that's about all I know from my mother's side.

My father's side, I traced it back to Mary, who was my great, great, grandma, who was the mother of my great granddaddy John, but beyond that, I have yet to recover. I was told that I'm kin to Louis Latimer, the man that invented the copper filament in the light bulb, so in actual, he invented the light. Louis was also a poet and a writer, so that where I guess I get my talent and prowess for writing from.

But for this chapter, I pay homage to my mother, grandmother and my daughter that I lost. Maybe, after more research, I will write something for my ancestors. I just pray that they are proud of who I am, what I do and the talent that they gave me. I truly don't want to waste what my families' blood sacrificed, earned and fought for.

You Lay Mae I

You lay mae I,
Again find solace and comfort,
In your gentle, warm embrace.
And see the sunshine in your smile,
Brighten the sweet apples of your face.
You lay mae I,
Hear the angelic harps of sound,
As the essence of your voice sings to me.
Calling my name, as only you can,
For you know that's where I want to be.
You lay mae I,
Nestle in that caramel glow,
That lies only in your eyes.
With the fullness of love that flows from them.
Cause there, I found no surprise.
You lay mae I,
Forever seek the abundance of your presence,
To cast away the rabid hounds of strife.
But each day I toll, I strive, I march away,
Till the grips of life release my life.
You lay mae I,
Keep you in my guarded place,
Where no hurt and pain survives.
For this is where we are safe, my dear,
Cause here, you and I are always alive.

Dedicated to;
Eula Mae Hamilton Latimer

OPHELIA

Now you're home, sweet lady.
You've done your work for your season, now rest.
Go, join hands with the Lord and be at peace.
Let the angels sing; "Glory to God," as you join
their fold.
You've done your work for your season, now rest.
We all felt honored to bathe in your glow of love.
Let the angels sing; "Glory to God," as you join
their fold.
Now your light shines exponentially more and
deservingly so.
We all felt honored to bathe in your glow of love.
Job well done, so take a bow sweet lady, as you
ascend above.
Now your light shines exponentially more and
deservingly so.
And only the Lord can heal the hearts of those left
behind.
Job well done, so take a bow sweet lady, as you
ascend above.
For you have left your mark on all generations to
come,
And only the Lord can heal the hearts of those left
behind.
We won't say goodbye, but through the Lord, we'll
see you later.

My World   **K. Charles Latimer**

For you have left your mark on all generations to
come,
As your presence will appears in the eyes of your
descendants.
We won't say goodbye, but through the Lord, we'll
see you later.
But for now, let me shed these tears out of love.

WITH ALL MY LOVE GRANDMA.

NEXT STEP

From birth we emerge, shrouded in the crimson
remnants of our previous cul-de-sac.
Being cleansed of such matter, one should move
forward, yet we tend to move back.
Infants learn, by screams and shrills, how to get
what they want and parents reply for their own
sanity.
Neither the infant nor the parents realize that this
is the birth place of human vanity.
Next step.
Still an infant, the seed of vanity grows, as does the
knowledge of wants and needs take hold.
Even though, parents claim to know the difference
between the two, they still fall prey to the fold.
This enters the mix, so they give the child what
they want that they may be able to go on.
The child learns quickly how to satisfy their whims,
but this is dismissed with the proclamation that the
child is stubborn.
Next step.
Now the child walks and talks to the joy of their
parents acclaim.
But as the child plays with others, the seed of
vanity grows and remains.
Then the parents hear the screams of; "Mine,
mine, mine,! They rush in and to their wonderer.

My World   **K. Charles Latimer**

Their child has entered the zone, fed by vanity, the
land of selfishness.
Next step.
Even though, this particular step I put last on the
list.
Its power tends to fool us through conquer and
bliss.
At a young age this starts to gulp and consume
most of the vanity that gives it worth.
What we see, as a youth. What we do, as a youth is
strengthen by the vanity from birth.
Our relationships, our successes and what we have
become, all derives.
All the while this beast is feasting off the picnic
table of vanity as it consumes us and controls us,
this is our pride.

MINA

Gone.

My child.

Sweet Mina.

A life too short.

A small gift full of love.

Go home my angel,

But wait for me,

Dear Mina.

I'll be,

There.

Everlasting Bond

What a glorious sight.
As family and friends join together.
Even though for this day, yet not only for this day.
This is a cultivation of love and blood that will last
forever.
See the smiles on the faces before you.
The warmth in the hearts all around.
It resonates, not only from their presence,
But from the echoes of their sounds.
The magic from this time of year,
Allows the true love of the world to shine through.
I may not be there with my family,
But know that my heart is with each and every one
of you.
Give glory to God for His presence in our lives.
Let His mercy and love sustain us all.
May we, not only be blessed by these gifts,
But in return, open our hearts with trust for each
other.
I pray for all a very happy Holidays,
And may all your hopes and dreams come true.
For in my heart, I gather all of you,
And sincerely say, I Love You.

Echoes of the Mirror.

Staring blankly, at the image before me, I resent
what I see.
The lips, the nose and the eyes that glare back at
me.
Then the image begins to speck with a voice I care
not to hear.
And my reply, to the echoes of the mirror, is a
conversation I want to put in your ear.
Image: *You will never amount to anything,*
   Me: If I listen to you.
Image: *You are stupid,*
   Me: For being in fear of you.
Image: *You can't do anything right,*
   Me: If I let you control how I do it.
Image: *I wish you were never born,*
   Me: To be and do great things.
Image: *You are ignorant,*
   Me: If I don't believe in myself.
Image: *You embarrass me,*
   Me: Because I'm better then you.
Then suddenly, the image became him gazing at
me with a bloody red stare of hatred, yet saying
nothing.
So I yelled, "Cry havoc, and let slip the dogs of war.
I believe you fear me more then I despise you.
I believe you hate me because I was you.

My World   K. Charles Latimer

Maybe you see in me your nemesis.
For whom better to defeat oneself then oneself.
Wisdom teaches us that hating oneself is illogical,
yet we are our own worst enemy.
So as you looked in the mirror and saw me, you
then turned around and saw me with an element
you didn't possess, compassion.
Now I look thru dark mirrored eyes and see thru
the windows of your soul,
And from what I see, you're not me and never
could be."
Then I turned out the lights and closed the door,
Not wanting to hear the echoes of the mirror,
never more.

What A Life We Live

What a glory to be in this world
Life gives us so much to be thankful for
We have the breathe that we breath
With that alone, what more can we ask for
What a life we live
Our kids are the generation to come
They are our legend, a door to our past
With them, we see ourselves and our wishes
We try to advice yet they refuse and cast
What a life we live
The strain to gain more education
Gets us a better position on this blue ball
Success makes it easier to survive
Given us the cheddar to spread to all
What a life we live
I love my life and all it has given to me
Even though I realize that money don't make me
I live because I love and give to life
And my mind's at ease and remains free
What a life we live
So worry not, if you have done your best
But your life is not what you thought
And the vision that you see in the mirror
Is not what you feel you have bought
What a life we live
Live, love and be who you are
Never change the heart that you give
For that's the true essence of you
What a life we live

Zeus.

What he knew wasn't taught.
When to comfort me was no trick.
A tilt of the head as I spoke.
Homing in to my frequency.
As my heart pains with whys,
His gentle paw pats my knee.
Heat of sickness weakened me.
A moist tongue licks my hand.
Coming home,
A welcoming tail wags to greet me.
Walks in the park,
He struts and gallops with joy.
My co-pilot when I drive,
A whimper sensing my weariness.
As I soundly sleep,
A cold nose of concern on my cheek.
His unconditional love,
Could never be questioned.
I can't explain the hurt,
When I had to say good-bye.
The look in his eyes.
Pained me to the core.
I cried, I cried, I cried.
Please Lord, I can't lose him.

My World   K. Charles Latimer

He's this man's best friend.
Ahhhhh! He's gone!
Tears rain in my hand.
Inside there's an echo.
I cried, I cried, I cried.
Do you know what he meant?
NO !
He was just a dog, I hear.
Do you know who he was?
NO !
He wasn't your child, they say.
No one knew or understood.
He was mine and I was his.
His love was sure but no more.
Good-Bye, Zeus.
I cry.

Chapter Nine

There has been an ongoing and rather heated debate about the will of man for over two thousand years. Many churches, as well as scholars, both theological and philosophical, have studied the scriptures, and they have made significate contributions concerning the human will. But before I continue, as the reader, we must have an understanding of the Gospels and a grasp of the subject at hand, only then can we speak intelligently about this issue.

Often the discussion about the theological thoughts of man's free will has been a bit distant and complicated, not only in opinion but in scriptural theory. This tends to leave most believers floating in a cloud of philosophical thoughts that seem to be more confusing than enlightening. So what I'm hoping to achieve is, not only a clear and concise explanation of this issue, but also to back it up with Gods own words from the Bible.

Let's start with the simple idea about man's ability or power of choice. This is a blessing that we have been giving by God, which separates us from any animal on earth. From the very beginning God gave Adam and Eve options and with those choices, even though they choose wrong, turn the whole world on its head. But who's to say that they did choose wrong? How do we not know that this was God's plan all alone? But I'll come back to this later, now back to the subject at hand.

There's a scripture that will help us understand our ability to choose. "I was mute with silence, I held my peace, even from good; and my sorrow was stirred up. My heart was hot within me, while I was meditating, the fire burned. Then I spoke with my tongue." Psalms 39:2,3. This is an excellent example of David having to choose between good and evil. When he said; "I held my peace, even from good," shows the fight going on between his members. He even made the physical action of not speaking. He said he 'restrained' his mouth, in verse 1, and with this he had to make a conscience thought not to speak. Then the wisdom to hold his peace again, shows a mental decision of choice. Every man has that ability to choose his or her, own words, to clearly give thought to what our response will be in even the hardest situation.

Then after giving thought of his choices, then he contemplated his options about what his response will be. "While I was meditating,"(some text use the word musing) "the fire burned, then I spoke with my tongue." So even while he was meditating, evil was presence, which means in order to have such a battle, good and evil must occupy the same space, the same thought process. This simply means that mankind has the faculties to select their own thoughts, words and actions. We have the option to pick what we prefer or what we desire.

In Matthew 12:33-37 "Either make the tree good and its fruits good or make the tree bad and its fruits bad, for a tree is known by its fruit. Brood of vipers! How can you, being evil, speak of good things? For out of the abundance of the heart, the mouth speaks. A good man, out of the treasures of his heart, brings forth good things and an evil man, out of his treasure, evil things." This verse speaks of the actual intent of our decision and even the origins of that decision. If the origin of our decision and action are coming from a good or bad source, then what do expect the outcome to be?

We've all heard the phrase; "He had good intentions.", but based on the previous verse, how can the outcome be bad? The better way to say this is that he expected a better outcome and as we know, our expectation does not always match our intentions. Because we can have bad intention, yet expect good results. Some may say; "Don't that work the other way as well?" I simply say 'no', because with good intentions, or fruit, the outcome will be good, even though we may not see it at the time. God will be God, no matter how hard we try to super cede Him. He knows the outcome and it will go his way. Again, we think that Eve made a bad decision, maybe with good intentions, but that might be the way God intended it to be.

Faces Of Self

Halloween, a fun, exciting yet morbid event
It a time where we can pose as someone else
A clown, a princess, a devil or whatever
We let another side of us come out
However, that masked other side
Is just something we try hard to hide
Yet on this day of revelry and fun
A comfort allows us to reveal it
But what we fail to admit to
That this cover on your face is the inside you
Through the year, seldom does it peek
Even though the disguise we don is what we seek
We bare many faces on a daily bases
And we wear many hats that others can't see
Whether demon or ghost that we display on this
day
Evil or freaky your soul makes a plea
There are a crowd of faces in side of a person
Our job is to admit that they live
Hiding them only feeds your ego
Revealing your true self is the sacrifice you give
So don't pick this one day to show your true form
For you fool only yourself in the 364
Hiding oneself from their true self
Heavy must be a weight that you bore

Una Tasza di Amore Pieno.
(A cup full of love)

Resist the devil and he will flee.
Then put to rest your fleshly man.
Take inside the tri-fold of eternal life.
Holy Spirit, Father and the Son of Man.
One thing I can surely testify on,
Is the love He gave to me.
His power is indeed to be glorified,
Remember His love is what set you free.
Mankind has a hard time dealing with love.
The love of God, more trouble then all.
In His love, He still understands,
Yet He loves you, even those that fall.
Are you tired of searching for acceptance?
Every avenue has been a dead end.
Raise your sights to your Big Brother Christ
In His heart he accepted you in.
Nothing on earth can compare to this.
God's love is a glorious force.
This is how you know His love,
He hallowed you with His Spirit, of course.
Sins have seemed to decorate your past,
These things, to Him, no longer exist.

My World   K. Charles Latimer

Years of trying to find happiness, peace and joy,
All this you will have, for in Him they consist.
Escape to our Saviors loving arms,
No matter what you have done or do.
No need to wait until you are better.
Deal is; "Come as you are," yes you!
Inside of Him your life will be change,.
Inward and outward, the same.
Giving you love forever to share,
Now go forth and proclaim His name.
How much more grand is God's love for you,
Ensue His love, I pray.
True love without bounds or delay.

The Way It Should.

Did you leave me lord?
Because fairytales are not always true.
But I believe that you are not a fantasy.
And what you say, you will do.
I wait and wait lord on your works.
And it seems like I'm waiting too long.
I know you will come in your own time,
But I need it now Lord, am I wrong?
He says; "I'll be there in my time.
Not when you think, but when I should be.
I love you and you should know this,
I'll bless you on time and that the way it should
be."
But Lord, my wife has left and my kids don't like
me.
My job is gone and I can't pay my bills.
I want to do your will but I don't know how,
In your life, I don't feel I have the skills.
Help me Lord, show me the way.
Take me Lord, show me when, where and how.
I am so willing to do whatever you say.
He says; I'll be there in my time.
Not when you think, but when I should be.
I love you and you should know this.

My World   K. Charles Latimer

I'll bless you on time and that's the way it should
be."
He says; "Trust in me and let me do.
I'll make your life better and free.
You will know that I am there,
Just trust and believe in me.
Let my power and grace shine on you
Just embrace and receive that glow.
For your blessing come from a far place.
From a space, you don't understand.
An element of pure grace."
He says; "I'll be there in my own time.
Not when you think, but when I should be.
I love you, and you should know this,
I'll bless you on time, and that's the way it should
be".

Dark Ghost

Look at me…What do you see?
Do you see an empty vessel, a soul-less being?
Do you see a shadow of what life is,
Or do you look beyond me without seeing?
How is it your existence mean more?
Or is it just a fig mentation of your imagination?
Does my humanly presence and prowess scare you,
Or does the thought of me slip pass your cognition?
How can you phantom this peak?
Where in the Great Book does it say you're greater
than all mankind?
Or is it the sole creation of your thoughts
And the mental superiority of your mind.
As my mother's gave birth, was that not real?
With the whips and chain, did not my blood bleed
red?
And even though your goal was to break me
With the destruction of my soul did I not still desire
to be fed?
As time has gone by you still turn from reality
Though great leaders have touch your life but you
refuse to see
How those cotton fields of the past,
Made you who you have come to be.
Many hundreds of years of our history
You dismiss it down to only twenty-eight days
This is the shortest month of the year

My World   K. Charles Latimer

And you expect me not to be fazed
Even today you give me your scraps and want me
to heal.
While you kill my young people, but I should
conceal.
Not appeal, congeal, and act surreal,
C'mon the naivety is lost, so let's be for real.
Sure the Head of State holds a certain power.
And with that title we pray by the hour.
But everyone knows the money pulls the chains,
A black face gains, but white money reigns,
Their effort to erase the stain, yet we still feel the
pain.
And they claim that we should refrain.
How…..
Dead bodies in a church, but we should search,
For forgiveness.
Blacks killed by the cops, but we should stop,
To find Kindness.
The road to justice is not only for you but for us.
It's weak by talk but grows by trust.
Not a request, but a must.
Not by you, did this land grow tall,
But by every race, it took us all.
So even now…., can we really say,
This is the U.S.A.?

Chapter Ten

As the saying goes; "There are two certainties in life and that's life and death." As I got older, not only did I understand this but have come to believe this. Death is a inevitability and is something that we must not fear but embrace. However, it is something that no one wants to meet soon and I always say; "Death, being an end, is only a doorway to a new beginning.", but in order for this to have any meaning, you have to believe in a afterlife. Being a man of God and a follower of Christ, I strongly take solace in a peaceful existence in heaven.

However, Mark Twain stated; "The fear of death follows from the fear of life. A man whom lives fully is prepared to die at any time.", and to me this puts life and death in the same category. Life is something that we never ask for, as is death, so if your life is lived good, fully and in peace then death, whatever you believe, will be in peace.

Just as most people, I haven't done all that I should've but I did my best. I didn't cradle my kin the way they wanted or needed but I did my best. And I admit that I didn't love the ladies that loved me the way that they loved me but I tried. I've asked the Lord for forgiveness and I believe he has but, at this moment, I ask for forgiveness from all that I have harmed, hurt and lied to.

This, at the time in which I write this, is not a death bed confession and I have no life debilitating sickness. Yet I put these thoughts on paper so that they will last forever. That maybe 20years, after I'm gone, some may look at these words and learn, live and love without making the same mistakes that I have with my family and love ones.

Humanity, as fickle as it is, we try, as best we can, to embrace those around us. Yet, the torments of life whittle us down so much that all we have to give is only what remains.

Shade of Trees.

Settle down, my child, and relax to the words of
the babbling brook.
Bend your ear as it whispers the subtle tones of
rest.
Listen to the soothing rhythms of breathe, as you
believe it's there.
And take solace in the tender grass that surrounds
you.
Imagine, at this moment, a sweet and loving kiss,
Of the morning dew that trickles down on your
skin,
As you have crossed over the river and lay rest
under the shade of trees.
If not for the inconvenience, it would be
convenient,
To skip among the grass while the moisture tickles
your toes.
Yet in your dreams, it is possible, because now all
things are.
There is peace in the valley and the countryside.
No longer are there mountains or hills to climb.

My World   K. Charles Latimer

"Listen close. Do you hear?" I say to those whom
my voice now only echoes.
"Like flowers, love is only heard when you shut all
things out, so you can hear.
Don't let the cooling moisture of the soil cover you
before you are able to listen.
Nor let the absence of your presence be the echoes
you want others to adhere."
Me, I waited too late.
Me, I didn't pass the plate.
So please forgive me for not being all that you
thought I should be.
Please forgive me for the pain I have cause for
being me.
So for these things, I am sorry, but for now, let me
rest here under the shade of this tree.

Here I am.

Nothing that you wish will change this moment.
Not a single prayer of resurrection will lift me
You have all joined together to lay me to rest.
With the hopes and dreams of all left behind, I see
But, here I am.
I tried hard not to harm those that I loved.
Also, those that filled my life with joy.
I feel I have fail in both elements, causing them
pain.
Even though my intention was to make them smile
like a new toy.
However, here I am.
Here I am, with my last words I say be firm
Lift up your dreams and til your last days hold
strong.
Let nothing stop you from reaching your goal.
If your heart is right, allow no one to say you're
wrong.
Because, here I am.
Here I am, and I will never leave you.
When times are bad, I'm here to cling to.
While in life, I wasn't always there to support.
But in death, I pray that these words comfort.
So, here I am.
My love, I know, I've never showed.

My World   K. Charles Latimer

To those, affection, I know I owe.
Even to my family, I had more to give.
With the abundance of life, that I have lived.
But now, here I am.
Here I am to tell you I'm sorry
With all the hopes and dreams of glory.
Here I am to say I love you.
Because you're never alone no matter what you go
through.
Here I am
Here I am

Chapter Eleven

The Mother of earth. The Mother of mankind. The Mother of all creation. She is the most cherished, yet the most hated and the most demised person on the earth. She comes in many forms, many colors and many styles. She is replicated, duplicated and copied, however, no one could ever be her. A Black women.

She is strong, she is powerful, she is independent and no other women on this earth that has gone through more. She has worked the fields, lifted the barges, toted the bails and still feed the babies, from her tit, those that held a hatred for her from hell. So all those that nursed from her has a bit of blackness in them, which they fight against every waking moment. A black women.

Not only does she bare the weight of this pain, she also helps carry the load of the black man, whom, at times, treat her worst then the white man that rapped and abused her from the start. To find a good black man is slowly beginning to be additional chore because the black men are becoming scarce and increasingly damaged by society.

Me, as a black man, I see and understand the plight of my sistas but I cannot say that I share their affliction. Being a black man holds its own struggles, to which our melatonin lacking counterparts, have yet to discern. But to be a woman, and a black woman at that, is a torture of worldly disrespect that shouldn't be laid on anyone.

So I get why my black sistas are as arrogant, impatient and angry the way they are.
I love my ebony queens, because there are no other females that are as sexy, beautiful, strong, dedicated and sound, as my African Princesses. I admit, I have been hurt by them and I also have hurt my share of them but I will never give up on my Black Goddesses and I hope that they don't give up on me.

These next poems are dedicated to and for my Nubian women of royalty, my bronze babes of beauty and my Golden goddess of greatness. I had a true queen named Kim and I messed up and lost her. I don't expect any other women to live up to her but I do want them to have her class, her style and her grace. No one will ever match her but getting close, is all I ask.

Real Me

What did I do to you, lady
Why did I break your heart
Was it because I didn't see your soul
Was it because of my natural goal
Did I just see your eyes
Did I just see your face
Was it because your lips
Or did I just see your space.
I'm sorry that I lost you, girl
I'm sorry that my eyes were lost in a different place
I'm sorry that I made you mad
I'm sorry that my minds was in a separate space
I hope that you can feel me
Because this is the real me
When I met you, my heart said this is it
But the man in me said look at those tits
With a body like yours
I couldn't feel much more
But with a mind like mine
I couldn't be for sure
I'm sorry that I lost you, girl
I'm sorry that my eyes were lost in a different place
I'm sorry that I made you mad
I'm sorry that my mind was in a separate space

My World   K. Charles Latimer

I hope that you can feel me
Because this is the real me
I really don't mean to be rude
Because I see you have a attitude
You are simply beautiful girl
Please let be a part of your world
Tonight, I'll be a vacuum girl, tell you why
Suck you so hard, till you get dry.
I'm sorry that my eyes were in a different place
I'm sorry that I made you mad
I'm sorry that our minds were in a separate place
I hope that you can feel me
Because this is the real me

Coal To KrystaL

We still believe we can wash away the stain.
But it remains, sustains, constrains,
And we are still left with the pain.
Maybe love is like a piece of coal,
Black, dark, messy and mystical.
But with pressure, time and patience,
It will produce a bright and lovely KrystaL.
Or is it like a mother or father,
Even a sister or brother.
No matter the deep cuts they cause, Why do we
make love so hard?
It's a simple thing to share.
The glow that beams from our eye,
Makes all around aware.
Yet we somehow find ways to destroy it,
To damage each other's hearts.
Leaving only remnants for others to pick up,
As we scramble to find the parts.
It's like banging our heads against the wall,
When we know it only causes pain.
Then, as the blood trickles down,
Nothing can replace the love for one another.

My World   K. Charles Latimer

What about a man and women, husband and wife,
Does the same rules apply?
Or do they go by the waste side?
Is it because we deny or just simply don't try.
True love, is taking your partner,
And putting them on the highest hill.
Not letting their light only shine one way,
But over the world, like it should fill.
But you felt that my purpose was to obey your
every need.
And my existence was only a speed bump in your
life's path.
What did I mean to your heart beat?
Only you can do that math.
I tried to be your rock, instead of your stumbling
block.
I tried to be the cushion, that soften the blow,
Instead of a weight that was hard to tow.
I wanted to work this piece of coal,
Be it black, dark, messy and mystical.
And I believed with time, patience and pressure,
We would have produced a lovely and beautiful
KrystaL.

Como atrapar un gato
(How to catch a cat)

Sorry, I don't mean to bother you,
But if you could give a minute of your time.
That's okay if you can't,
Because I've got five and I'll give you one of mine.
From afar, I gazed the likes of you,
Even from a distance, I must say, I was at awe.
When I'm done talking I'll promise you one thing.
Like a kitten, after its meal, you'll be licking your
paw.
Now that you're close, the body, the eyes, the lips,
I can see what all the fuss is about.
You are indeed beautiful and if I used such words,
You'd be worth me cussing about.
It's a great honor to meet you.
And I can truly say,
Upon bended knee tonight, I'll give thanks,
Because today was a good day.
If you don't eat cause you're watching your weight,
Trust me, I watching it too.
I might be skinny but I'll go on a diet,
Just to be next to you.
To meet a new friend,

My World   K. Charles Latimer

Is like a treasure chest of riches.
You don't wanna talk now, that's fine.
I'll be back.
No matter how many times you throw me in the
ditches.
So I suggest we save the time and trouble,
And let's get to know one another now.
Because the seed of friendship can't be sown,
Without first putting your hand to the plow.
On that note, I'll end this.
Giving you a moment to think this through.
But I believe, with confidence, it'll be a pleasure to
know you,
Also, it wouldn't be a waste of time for you to
know me.

Do You See?

Do you see what I see?
Brown eyes that mesmerize you.
An ebony glow that hypnotize.
Chocolate lips, ohh so tasty.
Your neck makes me slob.
Shoulders, I yearn to kiss.
Your arms cause me to shiver.
To touch your hand, puts me in bliss.
Do you see what I see?
Breast, like dunes of Easters delight.
As I go down, I can't help but to be intrigued.
Belly, ohh that belly. Hershey made it no better.
Your hips are like mountains of goodness.
Please, don't let your voluptuous thighs close.
I look up at those breast and my eyes are stilled.
Peeks of mahogany glory.
I wonder, can I get my fill?
Do you see what I see?
To the ankles and the toes.
Then south, I go back.
To the area that you cherish.
By now your pudenda drips.
My sista, your choice is my command.

My World   K. Charles Latimer

Love maybe far away,
Be proud, my sista and so you should be.
But at this moment we stand.
Do you see what I see?
Queen of life, claim your crown.
It's up to us to bring back what they hid.
Black men and black women, together.
We are the original, look what they did.
Do you see what I see?.

ONLY A DREAM

As she walks nigh.
Shawl flux like waves.
Strides, rhythmic in grace.
Strands of black silk teeming from her head.
Bronze statue,
Then creamy ceramic that explodes with life.
I breathe, what breath
It's gone.
Cognition lost
Speech stifle.
Reaching to touch
But her eyes still me like salt.
Dreaming only a dream.
I wake
She dissipates.
Another drink to sleep.
Please, I beseech thee sleep
Then she appears.
Allow me to abide here.
Never again to let the windows open.
For the noise is too much,
And the lady's gone.
If my slumber be cessation,

My World

K. Charles Latimer

There upon solace.
To behold her fetching smile.
I inhale her aroma.
The sweet moisture of her kiss.
I know I've returned.
For reality can't create her.
Dreaming only a dream.
I wake.
She dissipates.
Another drink to sleep.
Please, I beseech thee sleep.

My Fault Before The Quake

Is it a short circuit in my brain?
Or a dis-connection to my heart?
How did I become this way?
Knowing, I wasn't this from the start.
Something that was grown and cultivated.
This was my fault before the quake.
I allowed the distance, the loneliness.
The love before me, in my mind, I made fake.
Destroy the walls of my safety.
The soothing broth of devotion, I refuse to taste.
Like a coward, I ran from many loves.
Now, alone I sit, with a life of waste.
Something that was grown and cultivated.
This was my fault before the quake.
I allowed the distance, the loneliness.
The love before me, in my mind, I made it fake.
I had many thoughts that I loved.
But like an imbecile, I feared the outcome.
I believed in my love.
Yet my certitude, fathered succumb.
Maybe it was commitment I ran from.
Or responsibility that I fear.
Both, are a likely reason.
As I sit alone in tears.
I allowed the distance, the loneliness.
The love before me, in my mind, I made it fake.
Something that was grown and cultivated.
This was my fault before the quake.

Can A Man Really Mean?

Look deep inside and shine your light in every
crevasse
Seek for all the answers that will quench your
curiosity
By all means, leave no stone unturned
I willingly open the door for your scrutiny.
Lift the fingerprints and gather all the foot cast
Collect the D.N.A and photograph the damage that
has been done
Investigate, to your satisfaction and your peace of
mind, the destruction
Some are self-afflicted but the deep cuts are my
burden
You've been given cart blanc and nothing is refused
Just let me near to feel, to see, to smell and to be
with you
The doors are wide open and I've decided to hide
nothing
So let the skeletons fall where they may, for I've
got a few
Then search inside those tender places that you
possess

My World   K. Charles Latimer

And let me not fall prey to the; 'those before',
dogma
This, one hand, seems like the Lord's blessing by
divine decree
Yet, the other hand, has little faith in the Carm-ma
Can a man really mean that much to you anymore?
Or are we all automatically doomed to the pits of
the past waste?
Judge not, by the puddings label, for the proof is in
its contents
But in order for one to decide, one must be willing
to open and taste
"Talk is cheap," and "Words mean nothing," is
what has been said
However, by a simple word, God gave life to what
was once dead.

Chapter Twelve

In this chapter, we will look at a subject that is called; 'the end of day, the end of time or the end of the world'. There is a worldly view of this subject that take on a different meaning based on the religious belief. Even a proclaimed Atheist has an idea about what happens when the world ends. But here's the thing, everyone has an idea about the afterlife and it is just as I said an; 'idea.' No one knows exactly what transpires after we die, where we go or what it's like.

Since the beginning of time we have created stories about heaven, hell and purgatory, yet no one can say for sure who's right or who's wrong, so, we as humans, have a tendency to speculate. During this chapter, I'm not going to try to prove or disprove any religious beliefs or disbeliefs. All I will do is give you the facts in what is believed however, I won't go into a lot of details because this is just an introduction to my poetry.

Let's start with the theological word for 'the end of time', Eschatology. This is the study of the final events on earth and where the body and soul will go afterwards. This word derived from the Greek word eschatos, which means 'last' and ology which means 'the study of'. This also includes the study of death, judgement and the final destiny of mankind.

The Abrahamic believers hold that the end times will contain two areas, transformation and redemption, which means a rebirth or a transforming of the body from the physical to the spiritual, then comes the redeeming or cleansing of the soul. As you may know, to redeem something is to 'gain or regain something for a payment', and the payment was made through Christ.

In Judaism the end of day is linked to the Messianic Age and the Jewish diaspora. The coming of the Messiah is also a part, as well as, the resurrection of the righteous and the world to come. Some Christians have a similar idea known as the tribulation that comes before the second coming of Christ, which during this time, the Antichrist will engage in battle with Christ and all the true believers, will be called home to heaven.

My World   K. Charles Latimer

In Islam the appearance of the al-Masih al-Dajjal comes before the Day of Judgement. After the al-Dajjal arrival, which is followed by the coming of Isa (Jesus), who will battle the false messiahs and win, then this will lead to the events that bring forth the beginning of Qiyamah, which is Judgement day.

Now in Hinduism, the end comes when Kalki, who is the incarnation of Vishnu, come upon a white horse and brings an end to the rule of the current Kali Yuga. And in Buddism, the Budda predicts that his teachings will be forgotten after 5,000 years, which brings in an age of turmoil. Then the Bodhisattva, by the name of Maitreya, will show and reintroduce the teaching of Dharma and the final end will come through the sevens suns.

These are the different ideas of the end of time, none which can be denied or disproven; however, they are argued and battled over. Wars have been fought and many lives have been lost because of these beliefs.

But here's the irony of it all. What if what you believe is wrong, then where will you be? What will be your afterlife? Where will you soul, spirit or inner person go? Because with each vision of heaven, they each also have a vision of the underworld, netherworld, Hades, Tartarus or Sheol and if you have the wrong beliefs then you might

end up in one of these. I simply believe that a
spiritual, and not a religious, belief will serve a
better purpose. But who am I? I may end up in one
of these places myself. However, again these
poems are meant to help enlighten, guide and
strengthen you no matter what you believe.

Walk This Land

As I lay, resting here, my heart beat slows to a
calming pace and breathing staggers yet with a
soothing gargle.

Fear, worry and pain are not even an afterthought;
they are only has-beens and old friends that aided
me before.

My hands, arms and other extremities are
weightless with a translucent glow like a dreamy
aura.

Thoughts are smooth, like the ripple of the
Caribbean's, serenely carrying me further through
the oceans to the land of the great beyond.

Then slowly my eyes open to gaze upon the white
sand of a land far away.

Should I place my feet on this perfection with my
feet of imperfection, I thought, as if I had a choice.

I never dreamed that I had a chance to ever walk
this land, yet here I am.

Placing my feet, my toes tingle as the grains of sand
stimulate sensations in me I thought would never
be felt again.

My World   K. Charles Latimer

Nameless courage moves me forward, each step
gathering cohesion.
As I look back, I noticed that ever step I've taken
that no imprint is the same.
Is there a change in how I step or a change in me,
maybe both.
Either way, something pulled me forward not
allowing me to step back into a previous imprint.
Not sure of my journey I felt the robe of one accord
drape me as I walk this land.
Looking back again, I saw the calming waters
moving forward, as if to follow me, erasing my
prior steps of imperfection.
Turning my head forward I noticed a thick cloud
that hoovered before me.
Beyond it, a mighty mountain stood crowned by a
beacon of light.
Resisting the force moving me forward, any efforts
would be vain.
I walk this land with a smile and enter the clouds,
full of joy.

With Dreed

With dreed, I awake each day, yet I move on.
The endless repetitions of life weigh heavy.
I float through these moments girded by
emptiness.
Hoping necrosis taps my shoulder.
With dreed, my eyes look toward weariness.
Hands that only mold uselessness.
And a soul that marinates in pity.
As the gates of Gehenna waits around the corner
for me.
With dreed, I anticipate.
With dreed, I capitulate.
However, with dreed being the bottom, all I can do
is look up.
The depth of the hole seems indomitable.
And a journey that seems absurd.
As I look up, the light that shines extends a hand.
With dreed, the power of hope can truly be seen.
The pit is made brighter.
But your head must stay ascending.
To see the ladder of remission descending.
So with dreed, you take a step.
Without dreed, sometimes, we don't even see the
step.

Only The Dead

There are many tales that men tell for prosperity.
Building the path for fables and legends.
And with each passing century the story gets
bigger,
As the truth dissipates ever so slowly.
Sooner or later all that remains,
Is some places and some names
For only the dead knows the true story.
In my heart, I'm a strong believer,
But sometimes our faith is the deceiver.
Falling prey to the soothsayers of the times.
From the heights of Canaan.
To the fiery depths of Sheol,
No one has returned to tell the story.
Cause that's a tale only the dead knows.
Upon your demise, the case remains
Yet the essence drifts and moves on.
Whether Buddhist or Islam. Believer or not,
Only the dead knows the true spot.

The Watering Hole

As I sat, sipping my drink, I noticed a group of old
men that had gathered together.
This was not unusual because every time I came,
they were there.
I never thought or wondered what they were
talking about.
Neither did I give thought to why they were at The
Watering Hole.
But on this day, my curiosity got the best of me.
I grabbed my drink and slowly walked over.
Introduced myself and shook their hands.
After the niceties were over, I finally asked,
"Why do y'all come to The Watering Hole?"
One of the gentlemen stood and gradually walked
to me.
He put his arm on my shoulder and asked; "You
never heard the story?"
"No sir." I replied. So he guided me down in a chair
and explained.
"Centuries ago, there was The Well that the
forefather gathered at.
Really, all those that existed gathered at The Well.
Then a couple of groups ventured off and begin
their own places.
Which one of them became The Watering Hole.
Back then, The Watering Hole was beautiful.
There were three pillars that held it up. One Black,
one Gold and one Crystal.

My World   K. Charles Latimer

On these lay the foundational floor, which was
Onyx Black?"
As he talked, my imagination begins to spark.
So I listened more intensely, as he continued.
"The Four Cornerstones were black as well.
But the walls were colorful and bright.
Flavors of Brown, Red, Yellow and White.
Then one day a new barkeep, named Alabaster,
moved The Watering Hole.
He changed the rules and took the old men with
him.
He then pulled out the Onyx floors and replaced
them with Marble tile.
Painted all the walls white, as well as the
Cornerstones.
But he couldn't replace the pillar because that's
what held the building up.
Then he forced the old men to obey his rules and
to drink what he served."
So I quickly asked; "Why didn't the old men go
elsewhere?"
He gently smiled and said; "Cause there was
nowhere else to go.
Then after a while, the old men begin to drink what
they were served.
And they forgot all about the old rules of The Well,
applying only to the new.
Even though The Well was still there, the barkeep
made sure it was out of reach.
The drink he served was strong and made the old
men stumble about.

My World   K. Charles Latimer

If they didn't drink what he served, the employees
threw the old men out.
At times, some old men scratched at the walls,
revealing its true color.
These old men were tossed out to cessation and
the wall was painted white again.
Some old men were tossed out and they did even
drink.
Soon the amount of old men thrown out were
scads and scads.
Over time the forced drink was diluted and was
said to be something new.
A lot of the old men joyfully drunk it, yet others
knew.
And at this moment, that's the same drink you're
drinking now."
I looked at my glass than back at his and said;
"Aren't we drinking the same thing?"
Again, a broad smile appeared on his face as he
replied;
"You see son, I drink at the well but I come here
too. The difference is, I know what I'm drinking, yet
the question remains, do you?"

Chapter Thirteen

Closing

If you asked most people about three things, non-monetary, that they want in their life, I'm willing to believe that the majority will say; Love, Health and Peace. Love is something that we all need. Whether it's love from your family, from your friends or from a spouse or significant other, it's something that, as humans, we seek, we desire and in actuality, we can't survive without.

We have all heard people say, and we have probably said it ourselves, that we don't need anyone. Studies have shown that when a person spends and extensive amount of time alone age quicker, they lose the ability to engage in normal conversation, they grow more and more reclusive and their quality of life diminishes, as well as, their life expectancy lessens. Now I do agree with those that may say that God is with us at all times, yet God is spiritual and the human body and mind thrives on human contact, interaction and communication. And of course, not all human contact comes from love. Some of this stems from hate, jealousy and pain which make our desire for love and to be loved even more of a necessity.

Health is more self-explanatory. Certainly, without your health, makes your day to day life even more of a daunting task. Whether it's an illness from birth, a sickness later in life, something debilitating from an accident or just due to old age, we will all pray for a healthier existence. A dwindling health condition can indeed lead to depression and a lack of self-confidence, just to name a few of its side-effects. Our health is a major factor in our ability to move freely, provide for our families and enjoy life as we should and that's way companies make billions of dollars on the simple premise of health.

However, Peace can take on many forms. It's not always about being in a quiet place because all hell could be breaking loose around you but yet you are at peace. That scenario can even be the other way around. You can be in very quiet place yet peace seems to allude you. I'm sure that we can all relate to my previous comments. Love and health, at times, can take on more of a physical aspect but peace, for the most part, takes on a more mental and spiritual presence. A peace of mind, a peace of spirit and a peace in the heart and soul may show in your disposition but those that don't know us, most of the times, won't see the peace in us.

We even wish our passed love ones to rest in peace, not for sure whether they will or won't, yet we have faith and we can only hope that they do rest in that state of peace. Of course, the peace in which we hope for our passed love ones is the peace, whether it called Swarga Loka in Hindu,

Firdaus in Islam, Nirvana by the Buddhist or Shamayim by the Jewdist, that's the equivalence of heaven.

But, whether it's peace, love, happiness, good health or wealth, all of these are products of a higher power. A power that, no matter how much some may say they know, no one truly knows. All we can do is strive to know more and that's where, I believe, the reward comes from. It's not about conquering the mountain top; it's about the true efforts to get there.

Yet the opposite side of this is the hate, fear, racism and anger are elements of a negative force, an evil entity, dare I say, the Devil. But think for a moment, if you believe that the Devil exists then you have to believe in God and vise-versa. Because with all good things there is an opposite, a bad thing and one cannot exist without the other, Even though good outweighs bad and love conquers hate the two still occupy the same space. Also think about this, Pain and Hurt sits right in the middle of both of these because once you fall into this area, you're going to either fall into the pits of hate or forgive and rise to warmth of love. Maybe this is the reason why hot air rises and cold air descends

Well, I hope that you give all I've said some though. And that you've enjoyed this book. Like always, my hopes are to bring peace to those whom may read these for they have given me peace to write them. Thank you and God Bless.

www.ingramcontent.com/pod-product-compliance
Lightning Source LLC
Chambersburg PA
CBHW071612150726
48000CB00004B/1691